INDIAN MUSLIMS: WHO ARE THEY

By the same author

History of the Khaljis, 1950, 1967, 1980
Twilight of the Sultanate, 1963, 1980
Studies in Medieval Indian History, 1966
Studies in Asian History (edited), 1969
Growth of Muslim Population in Medieval India, 1973
Early Muslims in India, 1984
The Mughal Harem, 1988
The Legacy of Muslim Rule in India, 1992

INDIAN MUSLIMS
WHO ARE THEY

K.S. LAL

VOICE OF INDIA
New Delhi

First published, 1990
First reprint, 1993
Second reprint, 2004
Third reprint, 2012
Fourth reprint, 2018

ISBN: 978-81-85990-10-1

Published by Voice of India, 2/18, Ansari Road, New Delhi – 110 002.
Printed at D.K. Fine Arts Press (Pvt.) Ltd., Delhi – 110 052.

Contents

Indian Muslims

Prologue

There are books on Indian Muslims like M. Mujeeb's *The Indian Muslims* (George Allen & Unwin, London, 1967) and Ram Gopal's *Indian Muslims* (Asia Publishing House, Bombay, 1959). There are Journals, Articles, and "Letters to the Editor" on Indian Muslims or Muslim Indians. But who are these Indian Muslims?

M. Mujeeb answers: "whoever they may be, and wherever they may be in India, the Indian Muslims take themselves for granted" (p.9). It is indeed not necessary to attempt a meticulous definition of Indian Muslims because they are so keen on asserting their identity that one cannot mistake them wherever they may be. Mujeeb further adds: "It is the author's firm belief that the Indian Muslims have, in their religion of Islam, and in the true representatives of the moral and spiritual values of Islam the most reliable standards of judgement, and they need not look elsewhere to discover how high or low they stand" (p.24).

Inspite of this declaration, the moral and spiritual values of Islam and the actions of their true representatives, have been studied by many scholars in India and abroad, more abroad than in India. We shall therefore not concern ourselves with these values here. We shall confine our study to processes of how Indian Muslims came into being and how they have grown in numbers to form the largest minority in India. Ours is a study only in the demography of Indian Muslims.

July, 1990 K.S. Lal

Chapter 1

Early Muslims

No integrated contemporary account exists to say how Islam spread in India. Medieval chroniclers very graphically describe the achievements of Muslim invaders, conquerors, monarchs, governors, rulers of independent Muslims kingdoms, and even officials, in effecting conversions. Muslim hagiological works, some reliable others not so reliable, too report on addition to Muslim population through conversions. But the actual numbers who embraced Islam year after year and decade after decade are not known. Some Muslims no doubt came from abroad as conquerors and soldiers. Some scholars and religious men also arrived either in the train of conquerors or at the invitation of Indian sultans or as refugees. Arabs, Abyssinians, Egyptians, Persians and Transoxionians, all find mention as having come to India to seek refuge or fortune. But the majority of Muslims are converts from Hinduism. One has, therefore, to collect facts and figures contained in stray references of medieval writers, especially Persian chroniclers, to make a conversion-cum-immigration survey to be able to estimate the growth of Muslim population.

On a study in depth on the growth of Muslim population, one is struck by the fact that as against the zig-zag pattern of rise and fall of the overall population in the medieval period, Muslim population shows only a constant rise. Another is that in spite of centuries of exertion in the field of proselytization, India has been converted only but partially. This proves that in contrast to the quick conversion of some West Asian countries,

Islam received a definite check in India. In other words, while countries like Arabia, Persia, Mesopotamia and Syria succumbed to the onslaught of Islam and converted *en masse,* the sword of Islam was blunted in India. This check provided provocation and enthusiasm to some Muslim conquerors and rulers to take to the task of proselytization with great zeal and earnestness. Their exertions and achievements find repeated mention in official and non-official chronicles and similar other works. Sometimes, besides broad facts, actual data and figures in this regard are also available. All this information is very helpful in estimating Muslim numbers as they grew from almost a cipher.

By the year 1000 of the Christian Era the extreme north-western parts of India, in the trans-Indus region, had become introduced to Islam. As early as C.E. 664, consequent upon an invasion of Kabul and its environs (which then formed part of India), by Abdur Rahman, a few thousand inhabitants are reported to have been converted to Islam.[1] Subuktagin also fought against the Hindus and converted some of them. But all these events took place in the trans-Indus region, and we may, therefore, agree with Lanepoole in saying that in C.E. 1000 there were no Muslims in northern India east of the Indus.[2]

However, there were some small settlements of Muslims in Sind, Gujarat and the Malabar Coast. Parts of Sind were conquered by Muhammad bin Qasim Sakifi in C.E. 712. Whichever towns he took, like Alor, Nirun, Debul and Multan, in them he established mosques, appointed Muslim governors, and propagated the

1. Ferishtah, *Tarikh-i-Ferishtah,* Persian text, Nawal Kishore Press, Lucknow 1865, Vol.1, p.16.

2. Stanley Lane-Poole, *Medieval India under Muhammadan Rule* (London, 1926), p.1.

Muhammadan religion.[1] In Debul, for instance, he enslaved and converted some women and children, and left a contingent of 4,000 Muhammadans to garrison the place.[2] In Multan about 6,000 persons were made to accept Islam. Al Biladuri's narrative indicates that the people of Sawandari, Basmad, Kiraj, and Alor were converted in large numbers.[3] The reports of Muhammad bin Qasim Sakifi to Hajjaj also point to large number of conversions.[4] Caliph Umar wrote to some Indian rulers in C.E. 717 inviting them and their people in Sind and Hind to become Musalmans. It is said that in response to his appeal some people 'turned Musalmans and took Arab names'.[5]

Muhammad bin Qasim remained in Sind for a little more than three years.[6] After his recall not only the Arab power in Sind declined rapidly, but also most of the neo-converts returned to their former faith. Al Biladuri informs that "in the days of Tamim, the Musalmans (had) retired from several parts of India... nor have they up to the present time (he wrote in the middle of the ninth century) advanced so far as in days gone by". When Hakim succeeded Tamim, "the people of India had returned to idolatry excepting those of Kassa, and the Musalmans had no place of security in which they could take refuge".[7] Sir Dension Ross also says that "after the recall of Muhammad bin Qasim, the Muslims retained some foothold on the

1. *Chachnama*, trs. in H.M. Elliot and J. Dowson, *History of India as told by its own Historians*, 8 Vols., London, 1867-77, (here after as E and D), Vol.I, p.207.
2. Al Biladuri, *Futuh-ul-Buldan*, trs. E and D, I, p.120.
3. *Ibid.*, pp.122-24.
4. *Chachnama, op. cit.*, pp.163-64. Also pp. 205-07, 208.
5. Biladuri, pp.124-25. Also cf. *Chachnama*, pp.207-208. Also *Cambridge history of India* (hereafter C.H.I.) ed. Wolseley Haig, Vol.III, p.3.
6. Elliot's Appendix in E and D, I, p.439.
7. Biladuri, *op. cit.*, p.126, Also cf. Idrisi, E and D, I, *Nuzhat-ul-Mushtaq*.

west bank of the river Indus, but they were in such small numbers that they gradually merged into Hindu population. In Mansura (the Muslim capital of Sind) they actually adopted Hinduism."[1]

In brief, because of the efforts of Muhammad bin Qasim and Caliph Umar II (C.E. 717-24) some Hindus in Sind had been converted to Islam, but by the time of Caliph Hashim (724-43), when Tamim was the governor of Sind, many of these Sindhi converts had returned to Hinduism. Those who continued to retain the new faith remained confined mostly to cities, particularly Multan. After Mahmud of Ghazni's attack on Multan their number seems to have gone up for, writing in the twelfth century, Al Idrisi says: "The greater part of the population (of Multan) is Musalman, so also the judicial authority and civil administration."[2] However, up to C.E. 1000 there were very few Muslims in Sind.[3]

Similar was the situation in Gujarat. A military expedition was sent out in C.E. 636 from Oman to pillage the coasts of India. It proceeded as far as Thana (near Bombay).[4] About the same time expeditions were sent to Broach and Debul, but because of Caliph Umar's opposition to hazardous voyages, the policy of armed interference by sea remained in abeyance. Meanwhile commerce by sea continued. In the eighth century, Arab fleets attacked Broach and port towns on the Kathiawar coast.[5] Thus because of armed attacks, but more so through the channel of trade, foreign Muslims and indigenous converts began to be seen in the coastal towns of Gujarat. Ibn Hauqal (C.E. 968) observes that 'from

1. Dension Ross, *Islam*, p.18.
2. Al Idrisi, p.83.
3. See also Elliot's Appendix, E and D, I, p.459.
4. Biladuri, pp.115-16. Also p.415.
5. Tara Chand, *Influence of Islam on Indian Culture* (Allahabad,1946), pp.31-33.

Kambaya to Saimur is the land of Balhara...It is a land of infidels, but there are Muslims in its cities'.[1] Masudi, who visited India in 916, found Muslims of Siraf, Oman, Baghdad and Basra at Saimur (modern Chaul) besides others who were children of Arabs born there. There were Jama Masjids at Famhal, Sindan, Saimur and Kambaya.[2] All these facts indicate the presence of some Muslims in Gujarat. But their number was small. This finds confirmation in the fact that in an anti-Muslim riot in Cambay, in the middle of the eleventh century, only eighty persons had been killed.[3] Besides, the population of traders is by nature and profession migratory, and the number of Muslims in Gujarat does not seem to have been large.

Arab Muslims first settled on the Malabar coast about the end of the seventh century. 'These Arab traders who settled down on India's coast between the seventh and the ninth centuries were treated with tolerance by the Hindus', and so they grew in numbers. In the early part of the eighth century, Hajjaj bin Yusuf (who sent Muhammad bin Qasim to Sind), drove out some persons of the house of Hasham, and they left their homeland to settle in Konkan and the Cape Camorin area. Refugees or traders, Muslims were welcome in India, and 'apparently, facilities were given to them to settle and acquire lands and openly practice their religion...'[4] In course of time mosques were erected at eleven places on the Malabar coast.[5] But till the end of the tenth century their settlements were only too small. The Muslim Arab historiog-

1. Ibn Hauqal, *Ashkalal-ul-Bilad*, trs. in E and D, I, p.34. Also p.457. See also Istakhri *Kitab-ul-Aqalim*, E and D, I, p.27.
2. Ibn Hauqal, p.38.
3. Muhammad Ufi, *Jami-ul-Hikayat*, E and D, II, pp.163-64. Also S. C. Misra, *Muslim Communities in Gujarat* (Bombay, 1964), p.5.
4. Tara Chand, *op.* cit., p.33. Also Aziz Ahmad, *Studies in Islamic Culture in the Indian Environment* (Oxford, 1964), p. 77.
5. Tara Chand, *Ibid.*, p.34.

raphers, while describing the achievements of Muslims on the Malabar Coast, exaggerate their numbers and influence. They also miss to mention the Hindu reabsorbtion of neo-converts, for Sulaiman, who visited India in the ninth century, states that he did not find any Muslims or Arabic speaking people on the western coast.[1]

In short, while there can be no doubt about the presence of some Muslims in Sind, Gujarat and on the western coast of India, their number till the end of the tenth century was almost microscopic. In Hindustan proper, east of the river Indus, there were hardly any Musalmans in C.E. 1000.

In the year C.E. 1000 the first attack of Mahmud of Ghazni was delivered. The region of Mahmud's activity extended from Peshawar to Kanauj in the east and from Peshawar to Anhilwara in the South. In this, wherever he went, he converted people to Islam. In his attack on Waihind (near Peshawar) in 1001-3, Mahmud is reported to have captured Jayapal and fifteen of his principal chiefs and relations some of whom, like Sukhpal, were made Musalmans. At Bhera all the inhabitants, except those who embraced Islam, were put to the sword. Since the whole town is reported to have been converted the number of converts may have been quite large. At Multan too conversions took place in large numbers for, writing about the campaign against Nawasa Shah (converted Sukhpal), Utbi says that this and the previous victory (at Multan) were 'witnesses to his exalted state of proselytism'.[2] In his campaign in the Kashmir Valley (1015) Mahmud 'converted many infidels to Muhammadanism, and

1. Sulaiman Saudagar, Hindi trs. of his Narrative by Mahesh Prasad, (Kashi, Sam. 1978, C.E.1921), p.84.

2. For conversions at various places under Mahmud see *Kitab-i-Yamini*, Eng. trs. of Utbi's work by James Reynolds, (London) 1858, pp.451-52,455,460,462-63 and Utbi,*Tarikh-i-Yamini*, E and D, II, pp.27, 30,33,40,42,43,45,49. Also Appendix in E and D, II, pp.434-78.

having spread Islam in that country, returned to Ghazni'. In the latter campaigns, in Mathura, Baran and Kanauj, again, many conversions took place. While describing 'the conquest of Kanauj', Utbi sums up the situation thus: "The Sultan levelled to the ground every fort..., and the inhabitants of them either accepted Islam, or took up arms against him." In short, those who submitted were also converted to Islam. In Baran (Bulandshahr) alone 10,000 persons were converted including the Raja. During his fourteenth invasion in C.E. 1023, Kirat, Nur, Lohkot and Lahore were attacked. The chief of Kirat accepted Islam, and many people followed his example. According to Nizamuddin Ahmad, 'Islam spread in this part of the country by the consent of the people and the influence of force'. Conversion of Hindus to Islam was one of the objects of Mahmud. Al Qazwini writes that when Mahmud went "to wage religious war against India, he made great efforts to capture and destroy Somnat, in the hope that the Hindus would then become Muhammadans".[1] Sultan Mahmud was well-versed in the Quran and was considered its eminent interpreter.[2] He ardently desired to play the role of a true Muslim monarch and convert non-Muslims to his faith. *Tarikh-i-Yamini*, *Rausat-us-Safa* and *Tarikh-i-Ferishtah*, besides many other works, speak of construction of mosques and schools and appointment of preachers and teachers by Mahmud and his successor Masud.[3] Wherever Mahmud went, he insisted on the people to convert to Islam. Such was the insistence on the conversion of the vanquished Hindu princes that many rulers just fled before Mahmud even without giving a battle. "The object of Bhimpal in recom-

1. Zakaria al Qazwini, *Asar-ul-Bilad*, E and D, I, p.98.
2. C.E. Bosworth, *The Ghaznavids* (Edinburgh, 1963), p. 129. Utbi, Reynolds trs. *op. cit.*, pp.438-39 and n.
3. Utbi, trs. Reynolds, *op.cit.*, pp. 322-25, 462. Utbi, E and D, II, p.37 Ferishtah, *op. cit.*, I, p.44.

mending the flight of Chand Rai was, that the Rai should not fall into the net of the Sultan, and thus be made a Musalman, as had happened to Bhimpal's uncles and relations, when they demanded quarter in their distress."[1]

There is thus little doubt that during the first thirty years of the eleventh century, consequent upon the invasions of Mahmud of Ghazni, some thousands of people were converted to Islam. During and after his raids, a few Muslim colonies were also established, some in as far off places as Kanauj, Banaras, and Bahraich.[2] This is partially corroborated by the sixteenth century Lama historian Taranatha who refers to the settlements of the Turks in the Antarvedi or the Ganga-Jamuna Doab.[3] He further adds that during the time of Lavasena and his successors, prior to the invasion of Odantapuri and Vikramsila (1203), the Turks had increased in number in Magadh.[4] The traditional history of Maner and an inscription found there also corroborate the presence of Turks in Bihar in the twelfth century.[5] In Mahmud Ghazni's time some conversions had taken place in Gujarat and Kashmir also. Besides king Kalasa of Kashmir (C.E. 1063-89) employed some Turkish architects to erect a golden parasol over the temple of Kalasesvara. Another king of the same state, Harsha, employed Turks in his army.[6]

In spite of his great success the sway of the descendants of Mahmud in Punjab was precarious, and

1. Utbi, E and D, II, p.49.
2. About Banaras Ibn Asir says, 'there were Musalmans in that country since the days of Mahmud bin Subuktagin'. Ibn-ul-Asir,*Kamil-ul-Tawarikh*, trs., E and D, II.
3. *Indian Antiquary*, IV, 1875, p.366.
4. *Indian Historical Quarterly*, XXII, 1951, p.240.
5. Proceedings of the Indian History Congress, VI Session, Patna, pp.123ff. Also B.P. Mazumdar, *The Socio-Economic History of Northern India*, (Calcutta, 1960), p.126.
6. Kalhana, *Rajatarangini*, trs. by M. A. Stein (Westminster, 1900), VII, 528-29, 1149, cited in Mazumdar, *op. cit.*, p.128.

their proselytizing efforts could not have been quite rewarding of success. Therefore, the number of Muslims in the Punjab, like in Sind, Gujarat and Malabar could have been only small. Islam being a proselytizing religion, its followers have not only taken pride in winning converts but also often exaggerating the numbers of real or imaginary conversions. For instance it is claimed that in Gujarat some members of the depressed classes like Kunbis, Kharwars and Koris were converted to Islam by Nuruddin Nur Satgur.[1] But 'Nur Satgur's figure is one which is more legendary than real, at least in determinable historical terms.'[2] The story of the conversion of Cheraman Perumal of Malabar too is only legendary.[3] There is no doubt that the invasions of Mahmud of Ghazni brought good crop of converts, and a few more Muslims were added through the influence of Muslim Mashaikh and traders in Gujarat and Malabar. But if the example of Sind provides any precedent, it is possible that many Hindus forcibly converted to Islam during Mahmud's raids returned to their former faith. Very few Muslims were left in Sind after the decline of Arab rule. A local Karmatian Muhammadan dynasty was, however, ruling at Mansura and Multan. Mahmud of Ghazni destroyed it root and branch (1010) and Multan was deserted.[4] There was another wave of Shia immigrants. In 1175 Shihabuddin Ghori attacked, defeated, and massacred them; and the majority of survivors began to live in the guise of Hindus.[5]

1. Arnold, *The Preaching of Islam* (Westminster, 1896), p.275; Murray Titus, *Islam in India and Pakistan*, (Calcutta, 1959), p.43.
2. S.C. Misra, *Muslim Communities in Gujarat*, p.57.
3. Tarachand, *op. cit.*, pp.34-35.
4. Ferishtah, *op. cit.*, I, p.27, M. Habib, *Sultan Mahmud of Ghaznin*, Delhi reprint, 1951, p.34.
5. W. Ivanow, *Brief Survey of the Evolution of Ismailism* (Bombay, 1942), pp.34-35.

Thus while the story of the conversions to Islam has been very enthusiastically narrated by Muslim chroniclers, the attitude of the Hindus to conversion and the endeavours of the hurriedly converted Hindus to revert to their former faith, has not been even referred to by them. Alberuni mentions a number of restrictions imposed upon reconversion to Hinduism,[1] but he has probably noted only the extremely orthodox Brahman opinion. On the other hand *Devalasmriti*[2] and many other similar works[3], lay down liberal rules for the reconversion of men and women who might have stayed with the *mlechchhas* for even as long a period as twenty years.[4] All this points to a keenness on the part of the converted to return to Hinduism. We know that Nawasa Shah reverted to Hinduism at the earliest opportunity. There is also the case of Rai Sal.[5] Between Mahmud of Ghazni's death (1030) and Muhammad Ghori's invasion (1191-92) such opportunities of reconversion were many, even on a large scale.[6] Consequently, during this period of more than a century and a half, Muslim numbers do not seem to have shown any great rise.

About the end of the twelfth century, Muhammad Ghori established Muslim rule in India on a durable basis. When he captured Bhatinda in 1190-91, he placed in its command Qazi Ziyauddin with a contingent of 1200 horse.[7] In 1192 he invaded Hindustan with an army of 120,000. A good number of his soldiers would have been

1. Alberuni, *India*, trs. Edward Sachau, 2 Vols., (London, 1910), II, pp.162-63.
2. Published by Anandasrama Sanskrit series, Poona, trs. by M.N. Ray in J.B.O.R.S., 1927.
3. P.V. Kane, *History of the Dhramashastra Literature*, 4 Vols., II, pp.390-91.
4. See B.P. Mazumdar, *op. cit.*, pp. 131-33.
5. Utbi, E and D, II, p.39. *Camb. Hist. India*, III, p.47.
6. Ferishtah, *op. cit.*, I, p.45.
7. *Camb. Hist. India*, III, p.40.

killed in the sanguinary battle with Prithviraj. A major portion of the remainder would have stayed on in India under Qutbuddin Aibak, who must not have been left empty handed in an alien and hostile country.[1]

Aibak entered upon a series of conquests. He despatched Ikhtiyaruddin Bakhtiyar Khalji to the East and himself captured Kol (modern Aligarh) in 1194. There "those of the garrison who were wise and acute were converted to Islam, but those who stood by their ancient faith were slain with the sword".[2] In 1195 when Raja Bhim of Gujarat was attacked, 20,000 prisoners were captured,[3] and in 1202 at Kalinjar 50,000,[4] "and we may be sure that (as in the case of Arab conquest of Sind) all those who were made slaves were compelled to embrace the religion of the masters to whom they were allotted."[5] Ferishtah specifically mentions that on the capture of Kalinjar "fifty thousand *Kaniz va ghulam*, having suffered slavery, were rewarded with the honour of Islam".[6] According to Ferishtah three to four hundred thousand Khokhars and Tirahias were also converted to Islam by Muhammad Ghori.[7]

1. Hasan Nizami says that 'the Sultan then returned to Ghazna... but the whole army remained... at the mauza of Indarpat'. (*Taj-ul-Maasir*, E and D, II, p.216). Surely Muhammad Ghori would not have gone back all alone.
2. *Ibid.*, p.222.
3. Ferishtah, I, p.62.
4. Hasan Nizami, p.231. Also Ferishtah, I, p.53. Habibullah, *The Foundation of Muslim Rule in India*, (Allahabad, 1961), pp.69 and 334 (n.26), has missed to cite Hasan Nizami's assertion that 50,000 were enslaved.
5. Titus. *Islam in India and Pakistan* (Calcutta, 1959), p.31.
6. Ferishtah, I, p.63.
7. Ferishtah, I, pp.59-60. The authenticity of Fertishtah's statement has been challanged by Raverty (*Notes on Afghanistan*, p.367). The numbers of Khokhar converts have certainly been exaggerated. Amir Khusrau refers to Khokhars as a non-Muslim tribe (*Tughlaq Namah*, Aurangabad, 1933, p.128), and the way they were constantly attacked and killed by sultans like Iltutmish and Balban confirms Khusrau's contention. There is, however, nothing strange about Ferishtah's statement; only the figure seems to be exaggerated.

Ikhtiyaruddin Bakhtiyar Khalji's military exploits in the east also resulted in conversions to Islam. About the end of the twelfth or the beginning of the thirteenth century,[1] he marched into Bihar and attacked the University centres of Nalanda, Vikramshila and Uddandapur, erecting a fortress at the site of Uddandapur or Odantapuri.[2] The Buddhist monks in these places were massacred and the common people, deprived of their priests and teachers, turned some to Brahmanism and some to Islam. Buddhism did not die out immediately or completely in Bihar.[3] But Bakhtiyar's raid on Bihar did deliver a shattering blow to Buddhism and its lost followers were gained mainly by Islam. Muslim sway extended from Varanasi through the strip of Shahabad, Patna, Monghyr and Bhagalpur district,[4] and the presence of Muslims in this tract from early times indicates that conversions by the Khalji's warriors were common in this region. Bakhtiyar converted some tribes in the Himalayan foothills also, and one chieftain, known after his conversion as Ali the Mech, had exchanged his native beliefs for the religion of Islam.[5]

During the time of Qutbuddin Aibak a large number of places were attacked and prisoners captured for which actual figures or written evidence are available. Figures of any conversions during campaigns to Kanauj, Varanasi (where the Muslims occupied "a thousand" temples),[6] Ajmer (attacked thrice), Gujarat, Bayana and

1. The exact date of the raid is difficult to determine. Ishwari Prasad, *Medieval India* (Allahabad, Fourth Impression, 1940), p.138 places it "probably in 1197", Wolseley Haig (C.H.I., III,pp.45-46) a little earlier than this, and Habibullah, *op. cit.*, pp.70 and 84, n. 78 in 1202-03.
2. *Indian Antiquary*, IV, pp.366-67.
3. Fuhrer, *The Sharqi Architecture of Jaunpur*, pp.70-73.
4. Habibullah, *op. cit.*, p.147.
5. *Tabqat-i-Nasiri*, trs. H.R. Raverty, (London, 1881), I, p.560.
6. Ferishtah, I, p. 58.

Gwalior, and the campaigns carried out right up to Bengal are not available. However, since the notices of medieval chroniclers are usually full of exaggeration where figures of the defeated or captured non-Muslims are concerned, it would be reasonable to take into consideration only those which are specifically mentioned, any exaggeration being rounded off by those which are not.

I have calculated elsewhere that the numbers converted between 1193, when the rule of the Turkish Sultanate was established at Delhi, and 1210, when Qutbuddin Aibak died, and the immigrant Muslims were about two and a half lakhs.[1] To this may be added the Muslims converted, migrated and procreated since the days of Mahmud of Ghazni in the Punjab, U.P., Gujarat and the South. Thus by the beginning of the thirteenth century, there surely was emergence of a Muslim community in India. Structurally, the term community connotes "a geographical area with definite legal boundaries occupied by residents engaged in interrelated economic activities and constituting a politically self-governing unit".[2] Thus in a community is discerned a process of social interaction, interdependence, cooperation, collaboration and unification and a conscious sense of "belonging". In modern times means of communication have broken community boundaries. In medieval times human associations like family, relatives, marriages, class (or caste), status, and neighbourhood played a very important role in the community's life. Even now, despite modern times, it is to be noted that in rural areas, villages and smaller cities the community process is still more

1. K.S. Lal, *Growth of Muslim Population in Medieval India* (Delhi, 1973), p.108.
2. *Encyclopaedia of Social Sciences* (Macmillan, New York Reprint, 1949), pp. 102ff.

closely related to family, neighbourhood, religious beliefs and institutional factors.[1]

With this conceptual framework let us examine the structure and organization of Muslim community in Hindustan in the eleventh and twelfth centuries. Punjab saw the emergence of Muslims as a local community consequent to the invasions of Mahmud of Ghazni. But for a few immigrants in the shape of Ghaznavid officers and soldiers, the bulk of Muslims were converts from the indigenous Hindu population. Similar was the case in "pockets" of Sind, Gujarat, Bihar and Malabar. The process of their conversion was hurried. All of a sudden the invader appeared in a city or a region, and in the midst of loot and murder, a dazed, shocked and enslaved people were given the choice between Islam and death. Those who were converted were deprived of their scalp-lock or *choti* and, if they happened to be caste people, also their sacred thread.[2] Some were also circumcised. Their names were changed, although some might have retained their old names with new affixes. They were taught to recite the *kalima* and learnt to say the prescribed prayers. But beyond this, to them their converion would have meant little. These neo-converted Muslims lived, as before, among the vast majority of the Hindus. Their interest lay, as before, in co-operating with their erstwhile friends and relations rather than with their foreign co-religionists

1. *Ibid.*, p.105.
2. It may be noted here that Jayapal, after fighting Subuktigin near Kabul, "was contented to offer the best things in the most distant provinces to the conqueror, on condition that the hairs on the crowns of their heads should not be shaven off". Utbi, *op. cit.*, p.23.
W. Crooke in his *Tribes and Castes of the North-Western Provinces*, IV, p.226, quoting Ibbetson says that *chotikat* "is even now a term of reproach which is applied in the Punjab to those who have, on conversion to Islam, cut off the choti."
Also Hodivala, S.H., *Studies in Indo-Muslim History* (Bombay,1939), pp.137-38.

whose main occupation was to fleece the Punjab and exploit the people. They continued in their old professions and vocations; perhaps they were given some preferential treatment in the redistribution of the conquered land, but there was hardly any change in the economic set-up with its inter-dependence, cooperation and collaboration, and they remained as intimately associated with their old social and economic order as in days before they were made Musalmans. Situated as they were, some of them might have even tried and succeeded in reverting to Hinduism.[1]

But no community, however newly born, however weakly constituted it may be, exists without a moral power which animates and directs it. After the passing of a few generations, Indian Muslims would have forgotten the circumstances of their conversion, and developed a sense of oneness amongst themselves. With time, they would have begun to be considered a distinct and separate entity in the caste-oriented Hindu society. "The Hindus were so well organized in their social and religious life",[2] that a few conversions had not even made a dent in their social organization, and gradually they would have tended to become indifferent towards those who had become Musalmans, thereby creating in the latter a sense of oneness and cohesion amongst themeselves. As the influence of the parent society on them declined and the influence of Muslim regime and religion increased, the Indian Muslims began to look more and more to foreign Muslim ruling and privileged classes for guidance, help and protection, and in return gave them their unflinching

1. Ferishtah, I, p. 45.
Murray Titus, *Islam in India and Pakistan* (Calcutta, 1959), p.170.
2. *Ibid.*, p.8

cooperation.[1] Much more important than the recession of Hindu moorings and the ascension of Muslim beliefs and culture in their life and thought, was the fact that these Muslims were governed by a new set of laws – the Shariat. They prayed in a different fashion now, in congregation and many times a day. They began to marry amongst themselves. The magic word of 'Islam' would have given them a unity of thought, interest and action. Lahore and Delhi were their political and cultural centres.

1. *Chachnama,* mentions the case of a converted Hindu who could not pay respect to his old Hindu king by curtly declaring: "When I was your subject it was right of me to observe the rules of obedience; but now that I am converted, and am subject to the king of Islam, it cannot be expected that I should bow my head to an infidel." E and D, I, p.165.

Swami Vivekanand has aptly remarked that conversion means not only a Hindu lost but also an enemy created.

Chapter 2

Rise of Muslims under the Sultanate

Muslim population in India grew with the expansion of Turkish rule in Hindustan. Its rise was due mainly to the immigration of Muslims from abroad and conversion of Hindus to Islam. There were Muslim losses also, in wars, famines, and through reconversions, and there was the growth of Muslim numbers through natural procreation in years and decades. We study all these processes, to begin with between C.E. 1200 and 1400.

Muslim Immigration

In the armies of Turkish conquerors Muslims of many tribes like Khitai, Qara-Khitai, Qipchaqi, Garji and Ilbari came to India,[1] and they stayed on here. Fakhre Mudabbir writes that the army of Qutbuddin Aibak was composed of Turks, Ghoris, Khurasanis and Khaljis.[2] Thus in the early years of Turkish conquest immigrant soldiers comprised an important segment of Muslim population in India.

Also with the establishment of Muslim rule, batches of other types of Muslims began to arrive in Hindustan from Central Asia, Persia, African Muslim countries, and what is now called Afghanistan. India was rich and fertile as compared with their own lands, and with the extension of Muslim political power, many

---

1. Minhaj Siraj, *Tabqat-i-Nasiri*, pp. 238, 242, 247, 249, 256, 258, 262, 276, 281.
2. *Tarikh-i-Fakhruddin Mubarak Shah*, ed. Sir Denison Ross, (London, 1927), p. 33.

immigrants – soldiers and traders, saints and scholars, political refugees and adventurers, and even musicians, jesters and jugglers – attracted by the "abundance of wealth in cash and kind" – began to flock to India.[1] Only a few instances of such immigration may be mentioned. Minhaj Siraj says that people from Persia (and adjoining countries) came to India in "various capacities".[2] A great scholar of Iltutmish's reign was Amir Ruhani; he had come from Bukhara to Delhi during Chingiz's upheaval.[3] Qazi Hamid-ud-din Nagori had also come from abroad.[4] Fakhr-ul-Mulk Isami, who had been Vazir at Baghdad for thirty years but then had suffered some disappointment, arrived in India and was appointed Vazir by Iltutmish.[5] Nuruddin Muhammad Ufi, the author of *Jama-ul-Hikayat* had also come to Delhi during Iltutmish's reign.[6] Their important positions in India as well as the influence of the Abyssinian slave Yaqut at the court of Raziyah shows the presence of all types of foreign Muslims in India.

During the reign of Iltutmish, the Khwarizmi prince Jalaluddin Mangbarani fleeing before Chingiz escaped into India with 10,000 followers (1221). Even after his return (1224), some of his followers stayed on here.[7] Because of the Mongol upheaval, again, in the court of Iltutmish there arrived twentyfive princes with their retinues from Iraq, Khurasan and Mawaraun Nahr.[8] During the reign of Sultan Balban fifteen more refugee princes arrived from Turkistan, Mawaraun Nahr,

1. Ferishtah, *op. cit.*, I, p.84. Also p. 66.
2. Minhaj, *op. cit.*, pp.157-60.
3. Ferishtah, I, p. 66.
4. *Ibid.*, p. 67
5. *Ibi d.*
6. *Loc. cit.*
7. A.B.M. Habibullah, *op. cit.*, pp. 95, 97.
8. Ferishtah, I, p. 73.

Khurasan, Iraq, Azarbijan, Persia, Rum and Sham.[1] It appears that each one came with a large number of followers because Balban allotted for their residence a locality (*mohalla*) each.[2] These follwers comprised masters of pen and of sword, scholars and *mashaikh*, reciters and musicians. The fact that Balban had garrisoned the forts of Gopalgir, Kampil, Patiali, Bhojpur and Jalali with thousands of Afghan troops,[3] and in the royal procession 500 Sistani, Ghori, Samarqandi and Arab soldiers with drawn swords used to march by his side, indicates that a large number of foreigners had come to India during his reign.

The Mongols, who had sent central and west Asian refugees fleeing into India, themselves occasionally arrived as invaders and stayed on in the country. Some also came, as in 1244, from the eastern passes of Tibet into Bengal.[4] A large number of Mongols who had arrived with large armies and sought service under Balban entered into relationships with Muslim nobles.[5] In 1291, the Mongol invader Alghu "with 4,000 Mongols and their families", made India his home.[6] The colony of these neo-Muslims came to be called Mughalpura. Under Alauddin Khalji also many Mongol captives embraced Islam and settled down in India. According to Ziyauddin Barani, many needy persons from Khurasan, Iraq, Mawaraun Nahr, Khwarizm, Sistan, Herat, and Demascus came to Hindustan to receive bounty from Muhammad bin

1. Ferishtah, I, p.75. Also Habibullah, *op. cit.*, p.272.
2. Thus fifteen *mohallas* (localities) were colonized in Delhi. These were named as Abbasi, Sanjari, Khwarizm Shahi, Delmi, Alvi, Atabaki, Ghori, Chingezi, Rumi, Sunquri, Mosuli, Samarqandi, Kashgari, and Khitai. Ferishtah, I, p. 75.
3. Ziyauddin Barani, *Tarikh-i-Firoz Shahi*, (Calcutta, 1862) pp.57-58.
4. Ferishtah, *op. cit.*, I, p.70.
5. *Ibid.*, p. 85.
6. Barani, *op.cit.*, p.218. Isami, *Futah-us-Salatin*, pp. 205-06.

Tughlaq.[1] Ibn Battuta says that no new comer from Khurasan was allowed to enter into Indian territory unless he came with the express intent of staying permanently in Hindustan. Battuta was himself required to write a bond to that effect.[2] Under Muhammad bin Tughlaq especially, foreigners are said to have been preferred to Indian Muslims on important posts and their immigration encouraged.[3] Foreign slaves, male and female, too arrived from countries as far off as China and Abyssinia.

Then there is the fact of foreign traders and merchants coming to India in large numbers. They came both by land and by sea. Horse traders in particular came from the north-western side to Sind, Gujarat, Punjab and U.P.; some also came through the eastern passes into Bengal leading to the establishment of an Arab traders' colony in Chittagong.[4] It is said that the ancestors of Lodi rulers in India (1451-1526) were horsedealers.[5] We hear a little later that the best houses in Delhi belonged to the Khurasani merchants,[6] which shows that they had built permanent homes in India. Such was the position in North India. In the South, the coastal towns like Calicut, Cochin, and Quilon, to mention only a few, were hub of international trade. There were Muslim colonies on the West Coast from very early times. Indigenous converts added to the numerical strength of foreign Muslims. How quickly their numbers swelled may be inferred from the fact that when, early in the fourteenth century, Malik Kafur marched into Maabar (Malabar), about 20,000 Musalmans who had settled in South India for long

1. *Ibid.*, p.462.
2. Ibn Battuta, *Rehla*, Trs, Mahdi Husain (Baroda, 1953), pp.14-15.
3. Yahiya Sarhindi, *Tarikh-i-Mubarak Shahi*, pp.107-108.
4. Abdul Karim, *Social History of the Muslims in Bengal*, Asiatic Society of Pakistan (Dacca, 1959), p.147.
5. Lal, *Twilight of the Sultanate*, p.132.
6. Yahiya Sarhindi, *op. cit.*, pp.107-108.

and were fighting on the side of the Hindus, deserted to the imperialists and were spared.[1] During the thirteenth century Muslim territorial expansion was rather restricted. Till the very end of the century Muslim rule could not extend beyond what it had been by 1206. In the fourteenth century, however, Muslim arms penetrated into the south also encourging Muslim immigration. With the founding of the Bahmani kingdom, in the middle of the fourteenth century, the avenues of Muslim employment increased still further and so also their immigration.

What could be the quantum of this immigration? It is true that ever since the inception of Muslim rule in India we come across references to Abyssinians (Habshis), Arabs, Afghans, Mongols, Persians, people from Khurasan, Rum and Sham, and of course the Turks, as constantly arriving or living in Hindustan. It is also true that the whole atmosphere of the courts of the Turkish sultans was Islamic; all high officers were Muslim. Their repeated mention in the chronicles creates the impression that they were flooding the country. But repeated references to foreign Muslim elements may not have been due so much to their large numbers as to the important positions they held. It appears that the number of actual immigrants could not have been large. A somewhat detailed discussion on this point will follow later on.

Conversions

One important mission of Islam was to spread throughout the world. The Quran, the Hadis, the Hidaya and the Sirat-un-Nabi, the four all important works of Islam, direct the faithful to fulfill the above task. Therefore, "there was never any doubt in the minds of the Muslims of their right to spread over the earth...The *Hidayah* is quite explicit about the legality of *jihad* (holy

---

1. Lal, *History of the Khaljis*, p.250.

war) against infidels even when they have not taken the offensive...The Muslim Turks found the moral justification for their advance into India in the injuction to propagate Islam. As this could not, in the opinion of kings and warriors, be achieved without the subjugation of non-Muslims and occupation of their territory, the propagation of Islam became identical with war and conquest."[1] In simple language, conquerors and rulers converted people by force. It has been seen that during the Arab invasion of Sind and the expeditions of Mahmud of Ghazni, defeated rulers, garrisons of captured forts, and civilian population were often forced to accept Islam. Turkish rule in Hindustan was established in the teeth of Rajput opposition and the process of war and conversion never ceased. Malik Kafur, the general of Alauddin Khalji, gave the Raja of Dwarsamudra a choice between Islam, death or payment of a huge idemnity.[2] But under Muhammad bin Tughlaq there is greater insistence on the vanquished Hindu princes to embrace Islam. The most glaring example of this is that during the Warangal campaign all the eleven sons of the Raja of Kampila were made Muslims. Muhammad bin Tughlaq converted many people in this fashion. When Firoz Tughlaq invaded Jajnagar (Orissa), he captured the son of the Rai of Sikhar, converted him to Islam, and gave him the name of Shakr Khan.[3]

Ordinarily, captivity for a Rajput was out of the question; his sense of honour and the dire punishments with which he was visited in case of captivity,[4] excluded any attempt on his part to save his life by surrender. He either died on the field of battle or escaped. But in war

1. M. Mujeeb, *The Indian Muslims* (London, 1967), pp.67-68.
2. Lal, *Khaljis*, p. 247.
3. Yahiya, p.129. Ferishtah, I, p.147.
4. Alberuni, II, pp. 162-163.

civilians and non-combatants could easily be taken. Kafur Hazardinari from Gujarat or Hasan (Khusrau Khan) from Malwa would not be the only ones who were captured. They rose into prominence and therefore the circumstances of their enslavement and conversion are known. Large numbers became Musalmans in this way. Muslim rulers were keen to obtain captives in war and convert them. During warfare it was still more easy to enslave women and children. It was almost a matter of policy with the Turkish rulers and their commanders, from the very start of Muslim rule, to capture and convert or disperse and destory the male population, and carry into slavery women and children. Ibn-ul-Asir says that Qutbuddin Aibak made 'war against the provinces of Hind...He killed and returned home with prisoners and booty.'[1] In Banaras, according to Ibn-ul-Asir, Shihabuddin's slaughter of the Hindus was immense, "none was spared except women and children,"[2] who were destined to be made slaves. No wonder that slaves began to fill the household of every Turk from the very inception of Muslim rule in Hindustan. Fakhre Mudabbir informs us that as a result of the Turkish achievements under Muhammad Ghori and Qutbuddin Aibak, 'even a poor householder (or soldier) who did not possess a single slave (before) became the owner of numerous slaves...'[3]

In 1231 Sultan Iltutmish attacked Gwalior, and 'captured a large number of slaves'.[4] Minhaj Siraj Jurjani writes that 'his (Balban's) taking of captives, and his capture of the dependents of the great Ranas cannot be recounted.'[5] Talking of his war in Avadh against

1. Ibn Asir, *Kamil-ut-Tawarikh*, p.250.
2. *Ibid.*, p.251.
3. *Tarikh-i-Fakhruddin Mubarak Shah, op. cit.*, p.20 has "*jauq jauq ghulam har jins*".
4. Ferishtah, I, p. 66. Also Minhaj, *op. cit.*, p.175.
5. Minhaj, E and D, II, p.348.

Trailokyavarman of the Chandela dynasty (Dalaki wa Malaki of Minhaj), the chronicler says: 'All the infidel's wives, sons and dependents...and children...fell into the hands of the victors.'[1] In 1253 in his campaign against Ranthambhor also Balban appears to have captured many prisoners.[2] In 1259, in an attack on Hariyana (the Shiwalik hills), many women and children were enslaved.[3] Twice Balban led expeditions against Kampil, Patiali, and Bhojpur, and in the process captured a large number of women and children. In Katehar he ordered a general massacre of the male population above eight years of age and carried away women and children.[4]

The process of enslavement during war went on under the Khaljis and the Tughlaqs. Alauddin had 50,000 slaves[5] some of whom were mere boys,[6] and surely many captured during war. Firoz Tughlaq had issued an order that whichever places were sacked, in them the captives should be sorted out and the best ones (fit for service with the Sultan) should be forwarded to the court.[7] Soon he was enabled to collect 180,000 slaves.[8] Ziyauddin Barani's description of the Slave Market in Delhi (such markets were there in other places also) during the reign of Alauddin Khalji, shows that fresh batches of slaves were constantly replenishing them.[9]

Muhammad bin Tughlaq became notorious for enslaving women, and his reputation in this regard spread far and wide, so that Shihabuddin Ahmad Abbas writes

1. *Ibid.*, 367. Also Ferishtah, I, 71.
2. *Ibid.*, p. 371.
3. *Ibid.*, pp. 380-81
4. Barani, *op. cit.*, p. 59, Ferishtah, I, p.77.
5. Shams Siraj Afif, *Tarikh-i-Firoz Shahi*, Bib., Ind., Text (Calcutta, 1890), p. 272.
6. Barani, *op. cit*, p. 318. Lal, *Khaljis, op. cit.*, pp.214-15.
7. Afif, op. cit., p. 267.
8. *Ibid.*, p.270.
9. Barani, *op. cit.*, pp.314-15.

about him thus: "The Sultan never ceases to show the greatest zeal in making war upon the infidels...Everyday thousands of slaves are sold at a very low price, so great is the number of prisoners."[1] Ibn Battuta's eyewitness account of the Sultan's arranging the enslaved girls' marriages with Muslims on a large scale on the occasion of the two Ids, confirms the statement of Abbas.[2] Such was their influx that Ibn Battuta writes: "At (one) time there arrived in Delhi some female infidel captives, ten of whom the Vazir sent to me. I gave one of them to the man who had brought them to me, but he was not satisfied. My companion took three young girls, and I do not know what happened to the rest."[3] Thousands of non-Muslim women[4] were captured in the minor yearly campaigns[5] of Firoz Tughlaq, and under him the Id celebrations were held on lines similar to those of his predecessor.[6] In short the inflow of such captives never ceased, and it need hardly be stated that in the hands of their Muslim masters

1. *Masalik-ul-Absar, op. cit.*, p. 580.
2. "First of all, daughters of Kafir (Hindu) Rajas captured during the course of the year, come and sing and dance. Thereafter they are bestowed upon Amirs and important foreigners. After this daughters of other Kafirs dance and sing... the Sultan gives them to his brothers, relatives, sons of Maliks etc. On the second day the *durbar* is held in a similar fashion after Asr. Female singers are brought out... the Sultan distributes them among the Mameluke Amirs. On the third day relatives of the Sultan are married and they are given rewards. On the sixth day male and female slaves are married. On the seventh day he (the Sultan) gives charities with great liberality."
Ibn Battuta, *op. cit.*, p. 63. Hindi translation by A.A. Rizvi in *Tughlaq Kalin Bharat*, part I, Aligarh, 1956, p. 189.
3. Ibn Battuta, *op. cit.*, p.123.
4. Afif, *op. cit.*, p.265 has "*chandin hazar aurat musturat va makhdarat musalmanan nasib mikardand*". Also see pp. 119-20.
5. *Ibid.*, p.180.
6. *Ibid.*, p. 360.

the slaves, whether captured or purchased, became Musalman sooner or later.

The numbers thus captured and converted during the thirteenth and fourteenth centuries cannot be ascertained. But from the details given by the chroniclers, it appears that enslavement during war brought the largest number of converts and, as years passed by, they and their progency seem to have formed the bulk of the Muslim population. Only two instances may suffice to show how this agency contributed to the rapid rise of Muslim numbers. Bashir Sultani was originally a Hindu slave. He converted to Islam and became an important nobelman (Imadul Mulk) under Firoz Tughlaq. He purchased 4,000 slaves.[1] Later on they were all manumitted and married, and could have produced other thousands of Muslims in a single generation. Khan-i-Jahan Maqbul too was originally a Hindu. He converted, became Prime Minister, and collected 2,000 women in his harem. How many slaves he had is not known, but for such a high dignitary's household of two thousand, at least a few thousand slaves would have been required. The point to note is that all these women and slaves, if not originally Muslim, would have embraced Islam in course of time.

Proselytizing Activity of the Government

It was not during expeditions and wars alone that conversions were effected. For increasing the number of their co-religionists, Muslim rulers made free use of the governmental machinery in peace time. This was done not only by the sultans of Delhi, but by all Muslim rulers – of Bengal, Kashmir, the Deccan – wherever Muslim rule was established. Another step was the building and maintenance of mosques, Khanqahs and Sarais from govern-

1. *Ibid.*, p. 144.

ment funds. The buildings were often constructed on the sites of Hindu shrines and from materials obtained by demolishing them. These mosques, besides being houses of worship and centres of Islamic learning, often provided asylum to the needy and the indigent, who could be potential converts. Sometimes conquests were undertaken with a "missionary" motive.[1] Some rulers like Sikandar Butshikan of Kashmir (1394-1417) just compelled their subjects to embrace Islam.[2]

An important and effective means of obtaining converts was economic temptation or pressure. Ibn Battuta writes that Sultan Qutbuddin Mubarak Shah Khalji (1316-1320) used to encourage Hindus to accept Islam by presenting a convert with a robe of honour and a gold ornament.[3] In Bengal the landlords and Rajas who could not deposit land revenue by a certain date had to convert to Muhammadanism.[4] Under Frioz Tughlaq (1351-88) the state openly became an agency of conversion. Shams Siraj Afif says that he ordered his Amils to convert Hindus to Islam.[5] Firoz Tughlaq himself writes that he rescinded the Jiziyah to lure people to become Muhammadans, and this measure brought him groups of converts "day by day from every quarter."[6] And so were Indian Muslims made.

Contemporary sources do not supply any figures of the converted in this way. But the number of converts was perhaps not small. Ibn Battuta's assertion that Qutbuddin Mubarak Shah's system of proselytization provided a convenient handle to his enemies to murder him

1. Amir Khusrau, *Khazain-ul-Futuh*, English trs. by Mohammed Habib under the title *Campaigns of Alauddin Khilji* (Bombay, 1933), p.80.
2. Ferishtah, *op. cit.*, II, p. 341.
3. Ibn Battutah, *Voyages*, ed. C. Defremery and B.R. Sanguinetti (Paris, 1857), III, pp.197-98. Also Lal, *Khaljis, op. cit.*, p. 305.
4. Satya Krishna Biswas, *Banshasmriti* (Bengali), Calcutta, 1926, pp.6-10.
5. Afif, *op. cit.*, pp. 268-69.
   Also Ishwari Prasad, *Qaraunah Turks*, p.331.
6. *Fatuhat-i-Firoz Shahi* of Firoz Tughlaq, E and D, III, p. 386.

by introducing into the palace a large number of Hindus declaring them to be possible converts, shows that Qutbuddin was accustomed to converting large numbers.[1]

Voluntary Conversions

Side by side the efforts of the Muslim ruling classes was the proselytizing activity of the Sufi Mashaikh. It is, however, not known to what extent the Sufis were interested in the work of conversion, and this problem will be taken up in some detail at a later stage. Here it would suffice to point out that not many reliable references to their proselytizing activity are available in genuine hagiological works. They may have helped those who showed any inclination to become Muslims. Occasionally they resorted to force also to convert people.[2]

Closely related to the work of missionaries is the question of voluntary conversions. There are some references in the chronicles about individual Hindus accepting Islam because of dissatisfaction with their own faith. Al Biladuri mentions such a case. "The son of (a) king fell sick, and he desired the ministers of the temples to pray to the idol for the recovery of his son...But...the youth died. Then the king attacked the temple, destroyed...the idol, and slew the ministers. He afterwards invited a party of Muhammadan traders who made known to him the unity of God...and (he) became a Musalman."[3] *Tarikh-i-Tahiri* mentions the case of the younger brother of Dalu Rai, the ruler of Sind, who, of his

1. Lal, *Khaljis, op. cit.*, p.305; Ferishtah, *op. cit.*, I, p.127.
2. For instance Raju Qattal's efforts to convert Nahawan, the Darogha of Uchch; the latter's resistance and murder. Jamali, *Siyar-ul-Arifin* (Delhi, 1311 H.), pp.159-60. Also Ferishtah, *op. cit.*, II, pp.417-18.
Also see K.R. Qanungo, *Historical Essay* (Agra, 1968), p.151 for proselytizing efforts of the militant mashaikh in Bengal and Richard Maxwell Eaton, *Sufis of Bijapur* (1300-1700), Princeton, 1978, for the Deccan.
3. Biladuri, *Futuh-ul-Buldan, op. cit.*, pp.129-30.

own accord, became a Musalman and got married at Mecca.[1] Similarly one hoping through conversion to obtain his object of love, succession to property., etc, would have voluntarily embraced Islam. Some, whose relatives had converted but who were not prepared to cut themselves off from them, too would have followed suit. These are solid assumptions, often backed by references in Persian chronicles.

The 'groups' which converted to get relief from the Jiziyah, referred to by Firoz Tughlaq, obviously belonged to the poor, economically vulnerable sections. The few caste groups which converted to Islam did so because of professional and vocational compulsions. Such conversions took place mostly in urban areas, especially among artisans, mechanics, handicraftsmen.The Zamorin ordered some fishermen of Malabar to convert to Islam in order to man his warships.[2] Some urban tailors also converted. The inter-dependence of cotton-carders, weavers (*dhunia, julaha*) and tailors would have encouraged the former to embrace Islam. Beggars accepting cooked food from Muslims would have become Musalmans automatically. Butchers would have become Musalmans because their vocation found a ready and sympathetic clientele among Muhammedans.

Muslim Losses

Side by side the rise in Muslim numbers through immgration and conversion, there was decimation of Muslim population also. Muslim rulers had to struggle hard to preserve and expand their territory not only against Hindu Rajas but also against rebel Muslim governors and adventurers. There were wars against Hindu rulers for extension of Muslim political power and

1. E and D, I, pp. 258-59.
2. Titus, *op. cit.*, p. 39.

there were wars of succession and military campaigns against defiant Muslim governors. Withal foreign invaders had to be kept in check. All these processes entailed loss of Muslim lives.

A glance at a few historical events can give an idea of this loss. During the first year of their conquest the Muslims had captured Ajmer, Hansi, Kuhram, Sarsuti, Baran, Meerut, Kol and Ranthambhor. But in 1193 the Chauhan prince Hariraja, "collected a Rajput force and besieged Ranthambhor where, earlier in the year, Aibak had placed a garrison under Qivam-ul-Mulk".[1] The Chauhans also occupied Ajmer. In 1194 Aibak is stated to have crossed the Jumna a second time to capture Kol, but the next year again he had to proceed to the relief of its garrison. On his return to Delhi in 1195 "news arrived of fresh trouble in Ajmer," which was again besieged by the Rajputs in 1195 and Aibak had to fight hard for its relief; and it could be saved only by the timely arrival of reinforcements from Ghazni.[2] But a little later, in Ghazni itself Yaldoz was creating trouble for the Delhi Sultan. Such troubles recurred constantly; as a consequence of which there was loss of Muslim numbers. The best instances of such losses are found in the east where Bakhtiyar Khalji's ambition to conquer "Tibet and China" destroyed his whole army,[3] or in the west where a Hindu king, after defeating a Muslim army shorly after the initial Turkish conquest, openly regarded himself as restoring to India its original name of *Aryavarta* by killing off the *mlechchhas*.[4]

1. Habibullah, *op. cit.*, p. 63. Fakhr-i-Mudabbir, *op. cit.*, p.22.
2. Habibullah, 64-67.
3. Minhaj, *op. cit.*, pp. 152-157.
4. R.C.Majumdar, "Study of Indian History" in the *Journal of The Bombay Branch of the Asiatic Society of Bengal*, 1957, p. 150.

Sultan Iltutmish's accession (1210) was resisted by Delhi *Jandars,* and in the battle he "put most of their horsemen" to the sword. His wars with Yaldoz and Qubacha again must have meant depletion of Muslim numbers (fighting on both sides) continually. In his attack on Malwa – Vidisha, Ujjain etc., again some Muslim soldiers would have perished. During his attack on Nagda, the capital of the Guhilots, he was driven away by its ruler Kshetra Singh, with heavy losses. But the most interesting fact is that Kalinjar, Gwalior, Ranthambhor and even Badaon and Kanauj, which had been captured earlier, had to be reconquered by him.[1] Obviously the Muslim garrisons in these places had been destroyed by the Rajputs. Minhaj Siraj makes mention of a Hindu Raja of Avadh, Bartu (?) by name, "under whose hands and sword (in 1226) more than 120,000 Musalmans had received martyrdom".[2] The figure may be inflated, but the fact is important. Raziyah's rule was full of bloodshed. Armies of Delhi, Lahore, Bhatinda and Sirhind were involved in war. Karmatians had created trouble in Iltutmish's reign: in Raziyah's reign a thousand of them openly attacked the Muslims in the Jama Masjid, killed many of them and then were themselves killed. Ranthambhor had once again to be evacuated during her reign. Since perhaps during the period of the early sultans there was not muh Indianisantion of the army, the losses in war may have been mainly of the Muslims. Alauddin Masu'd Shah had acquired the habit of seizing and killing his nobles[3] (and certainly other Muslims too). In Nasiruddin's reign two attempts on Ranthambhor (1248, 1259) seem to have been made without success[4] but surely entailing loss of Muslim

1. Habibullah, *op. cit.*, pp.100-104.
2. Minhaj, E and D, II, p.329. Also . D.C. Ganguly in *The Struggle For Empire*, Bharatiya Vidya Bhavan (Bombay), p.55.
3. *Ibid.*, Minhaj, p. 345.
4. *Ibid.*, pp. 349,368-69.

soldiers. In wars in Avadh, Narwar, Gwalior, Chanderi, Malwa etc., again, many Muslims would have lost their lives

Add to these losses the Mongol killings in India. In 1241 the Mongols under Tair Bahadur captured Lahore, "slaughtered the Muhammadans and made their dependents captive".[1] Hasan Qarlugh wrested Multan in 1245 and "the whole of Sindh was lost to the Mongols."[2] It was recovered by Ulugh Khan (Balban) but the next year the Mongols[3] again arrived under Sali Bahadur. By 1254, the territory up to and including Lahore had been taken by them. During Balban's reign the Mongol pressure increased all the more. His son, the Prince Martyr, lost his life fighting them. So great was the loss on this occasion, that according to Amir Khusrau, "in Multan, in every house there was some dead to be wept for."[4] Vigorous Mongol attacks[5] continued right up to the first decade of the fourteenth century; and this alone can give an idea of the losses suffered by Muslim (and Hindu) population.

Meanwhile fighting at home never ceased. Balban did not mount any major attacks on neighbouring rulers, but even so his campaigns against the rebellious Bengal and Mewat would have only added to the depletion of Muslim numbers. Barani says that the Mewatis had killed a hundred thousand of his personal troops.[6] Jalaluddin Khalji's accession was attended by loss of Muslim lives. What Ranthambhor meant to him (and had surely meant to his predecessors too), is candidly confessed by him. He had marched to it in 1291, but recoiled from attacking it because he feared that its capture would entail great loss

1. Minhaj, pp.. 340-41.
2. Habibullah, *op.cit.*, p. 213.
3. *Ibid.*, p. 215.
4. Wahid Mirza, *Life and Works of Amir Khusrau* (Calcutta, 1935), p. 63.
5. Habibullah, *op. cit.*, pp.216-25.
6. Barani, *op. cit..*, p.57.

of Muslim lives.[1] With murdering Mongols he purchased peace. Although Alauddin Khalji rarely suffered defeat, yet there is no doubt that Muslim soldiers lost their lives in good numbers in the Bengal campaign, at Ranthambhor and Chittor and against the recurring terrific Mongol invasions.[2] The rebellions of Ikat Khan, Haji Maula and Umar and Mangu Khan too would have killed many Muslims. The massacres of neo-Muslims under Balban and Alauddin (30,000 under Alauddin only) would have added to the depreciation of Muslim numbers, and so also in Ghayasuddin Tughlaq's expeditions to Warangal, Jajnagar, Tirhut, and Bengal.

Muslim blood was shed most recklessly under Muhammad bin Tughlaq. Many of his schemes were costly in terms of human life. In the 'Qarachal' venture 100,000 soldiers are said to have perished. Many of these, if not all, would have been Muslims. A modern historian recounts twenty-two rebellions during his reign, twenty of which were of Muslim nobles or governors, and the details point to loss of Muslim lives on both sides, rebel as well as royalist.[3] During the transfer of the capital, according to the same scholar, it were mainly Muslims who were asked to go from Delhi to Devagiri, and it is they who suffered and died in the exodus.[4] Ibn Battuta and Ferishtah credit this Sultan with a love for shedding blood. Not a little of this blood was Muslim.

Under Muhammad Tughlaq's successor Firoz Tughlaq, Shams Siraj Afif notices a demographic recovery.[5] When he wrote about it, he was naturally thinking in terms of his co-religionists also. But after Firoz's death civil wars and other disorders began to

---

1. *Ibid.*, p.213.
2. Lal, *Khaljis, op. cit..*, p.144, n.66.
3. Mahdi Husain, *Tughlaq Dynasty* (Calcutta, 1963), pp.195-257.
4. *Ibid.*, pp.144-64, esp.149.
5. Afif, *op. cit.*, pp.95, 99, 264-65, 321.

decimate Muslim numbers. Most of the 180,000 slaves were done away with by his son Nasiruddin Muhammad Shah.[1] Muhammad Bihamad Khani gives vivid details of how with the weakening of the Sultanate, Muslim forces were repeatedly defeated and destroyed by even local ruelrs like Adharan and Sumer, and how Muslims were ousted from Chandwar, Bhongaon, Bercha, Kalpi and many other places, of course with great losses in men.[2] As the fourteenth century closed, Timur arrived to kill indiscriminately, not only Hindus but also Muslims.[3] Muslim numbers would also have contributed their share to famines, pestilences etc. commonly recurring in India.

Natural Growth of Muslim Population

These contradictory scenes in Muslim demography apart, about one thing one can be sure. While the overall demographic trend of India showed a decline, the Muslim population showed only an upward tendency. It is true that many a time statistical victories through conversions were scored off by losses in wars, yet an overall rise in Muslim population – sometimes slow, at others accelerated – is clearly discernible.

The rise seems to be slow between 1200 and 1300, and rapid between 1300 to 1400. Historical facts vouch for this behaviour. Up to the end of the thirteenth century, government effort towards proselytization is hesitant.[4] For example, when some Ulema approached Iltutmish and suggested to him to confront the Hindus with a choice between Islam and death, Nizam-ul-Mulk Junaidi, the Wazir, replied: "But at the moment in India...the Muslims

1. Muhammad Bihamad Khani, *Tarikh-i-Muhammadi*, 425b, trs. Rizvi, *op. cit.*, p.233.
2. *Ibid.*, fols. 418b-419b, and corresponding pp.228-29 in Rizvi.
3. Lal, *Twilight*, *op. cit.*, pp.17-43, 320.
4. Barani, pp. 42-44.

are so few that they are like salt (in a large dish). If the above orders are to be applied...the Hindus might combine...and the Muslims would be too few in number to suppress (them). However, after a few years when in the Capital and in the regions and the small towns, the Muslims are well established and the troops are larger, it will be possible to give Hindus, the choice of 'death' or 'Islam'."[1] Iltutmish, Balban and Alauddin Khalji were practical administrators, and but for the captives and converts obtained by them during wars, they did not act as royal missionaries. Besides, with the Hindus politically strongly entrenched right up to the end of the thirteenth century, Muslim proselytizing activity had to be cautious. Alauddin subdued the major Hindu powers. With their submission and extension of Muslim political power to most parts of the country Hindu vulnerability to proselytization increased. Therefore, between 1300 to 1400, under Qutbuddin Mubarak, Muhammad and Firoz Tuhglaq, conversions were effected at an accelerated pace, and immigrants also arrived in larger numbers.

In brief till about the end of the thirteenth century, Muslims in India were only like 'salt in a large dish'. The main reason for this phenomenon was that during the whole century there was little Muslim territorial expansion. To what had been acquired by 1206, nothing substantial was added till about 1300, and all the energies of the Sultanate were concentrated on preserving their acquisitions rather than expanding territorially. Such a situation was discouraging both to proselytization and even immigration. Even in the capital city of Delhi and its environs the Muslims were few, a fact which probably made Barani suffer from an incurable Hindu-phobia.[2]

1. Ziyauddin Barani, *Sana-i-Muhammadi,* Medieval India Quarterly, I, pt. III, pp. 100-105.
2. Barani, pp.41-42, 44 and 216-17. Similar sentiments are expressed on pp.72-75.

From the time of Alauddin Khalji, however, Muslim population in India began to grow a little faster due to the spreading of the Muslim rule to almost the whole of India after 1300, and it is rightly claimed that the establishment of the Vijayanagar Empire in the South was effected with a view to preserve Hinduism from the onslaughts of Islam. But contemporaneously the Bahmani kingdom of the South was also founded and it took to proselytising work usual with a Muslim regime.

By the close of the fourteenth century, the situation was like this. Kashmir's introduction to Islam had started since the days of Mahmud of Ghazni. Sind and Punjab were being effectively Islamised by rulers and Mongol invaders. In Gujarat, Deccan and Malwa also, because of the campaigns of local Muslim rulers against Hindu chiefs, the number of Muslims had risen. By the last years of the century, in the heartland of Muslim power, Muslim population of Delhi and its adjoining regions rose greatly, a fact which prompted Afif to write "from the *qasba* of Indrapat (present Indraprastha Estate) to the Kaushik-i-Shikar (present Delhi University area), five *kos* apart all the land was occupied......There were eight public mosques, and one private mosque...The public mosques were each large enough to accommodate 10,000 suppliants".[1] This clearly indicates a fairly large Muslim population in the capital city.

There is yet another, though indirect and not unimpeachable, evidence for this rise. Alauddin Khalji had abolished the jagir system, lest local officials should turn contumacious. But by the time of Firoz Tughlaq the number of dependable Muslims (or Muslims of a few generations) had increased, and he could safely entrust jagirs to them, "and during the forty years of his reign he devoted himself to generosity and the benefit of

1. Afif., p.135.

Musalmans, by distributing villages and lands among his followers" in lieu of salary.[1]

Indian Muslims around C.E. 1400

So, between C.E. 1200 and 1400 especially in the fourteenth century, Muslim population had grown at an accelerated pace. The agencies which contributed to this growth are well-known. Historical facts giving an idea of this rise too are on record. But the quantum or percentage of rise during the thirteenth and fourteenth centuries is not possible to estimate with any amount of accuracy for want of specific data. However, it has been estimated by me elsewhere that there were more than thirty lakh Muslims in India around the year 1400 C.E.[2] These Indian Muslims were not a coalesced lot. The Musalmans of Gujarat, Malabar or Bihar had little communication among themselves. The interests of merchants were different from the other classes. Even in the Central region of Delhi-Agra Muslims had broken up into groups of vested interests. In theory all Muslims are equal; in practice some have always been more equal than the others. Foreign Muslims tried to dominate over Indian Muslims. At the top were the Ulema or the learned, nobles and army commanders. They were all foreigners or descended from migrant Muslims. It was from the Ulema class that the high officers of government as well as religious institutions were chosen. Their presence was indispensable to a Sultan, who was generally uneducated, if not unlettered. They assisted him in the interpretation and execution of the law. It was through these men that the regime systematized the religious and social life of the Muslim community just as it organized the extension and administration of Muslim dominions in India through the nobility.

1. Afif, *op. cit.*, p. 95.
2. K.S. Lal, *Growth of Muslim Population*, pp. 125-26.

The nobility laid the foundation of Muslim rule in India. It was also sustained by the endeavours and exertions of foreign warriors and nobles. These foreign nobles belonged to Turkic, Persian, Arab, Afghan, Mongol, Abyssinian and Egyptian stocks but were known by the generic title "Turk". They constituted the ruling oligarchy of the early Sultanate. They were army commanders-cum-civil administrators, officers in charge of provinces and districts and holders of other similar appointments of various grades and ranks. Many of them had risen from humble beginnings; some of them were originally slaves. But conquest of Indian kingdoms had proved to be very lucrative. So greatly had they benefited during campaigns and wars, and so great was their need to hold and administer the newly acquired territories, that they all became men of power and influence. They were known by the generic term Turks and they insisted on monopolizing all key posts and important positions, and maintaining their racial and exotic identity. This attitude was also shared by their children and children's children, who though born in India, psychologically felt that they were Turks of foreign stock. On the other hand the foreign Muslims treated the Indian Muslim converts with contempt. They were so class conscious that Ziyauddin Barani, who was born in India but belonged to a family of nobles, credits the Turks, both in his *Tarikh-i-Firoz Shahi* as well as *Fatawa-i-Jahandari*, with all possible virtues and the Indian Muslims with all kinds of vices.

The Indian converted Muslims manned the subordinate occupations. The socially rejected tradesmen were weighers, camel and donkey drivers, changers, falconers, cuppers, leather-workers and tanners, geomancers, jugglers, and barbers.[1] The menials included scavengers,

1. Ira Mervin Lapidus, *Muslim Cities in the Later Middle Ages* (Cambridge, Mass., 1967), p. 83.

entertainers, funeral workers. Wrestlers, clowns, players, story tellers, and singing women, moving about in the streets, irregularly employed, knocking about for a living, associated with vice and begging, were part of this low class.[1] Tailors, weavers and carpenters were a little better off. Somewhere in between can be placed saddlers, bow-makers, blacksmiths, rope-makers, butchers, wool-dealers, bakers, gardeners, domestic slaves, beggars, labourers and pedlars of all kinds.

These professions were almost exclusively manned by backward classes neo-converts. Conversion to Islam did not change their status, and foreign Muslims looked down upon them. The foreigners especially were not prepared to treat them on equal terms at all. To add insult to injury, the chronicler Ziya Barani, a confirmed believer in the racial superiority of the so-called Turks and baseness of the Indian Muslims, recommends: "Teachers of every kind are to be sternly ordered not to thrust precious stones down the throats of dogs....that is, to the mean, the ignoble, the worthless. To shopkeepers and the low born they are to teach nothing more than the rules about prayer, fasting, religious charity and the Hajj pilgrimage along with some chapters of the Quran and some doctrines of the faith without which their religion cannot be correct and valid prayers are not possible. They are to be instructed in nothing more. They are not to be taught reading and writing for plenty of disorders arise owing to the skill of the low-born in knowledge..."[2] "The low-born, who have been enrolled for practising the baser arts and the meaner professions, are capable only of vices...."[3] Indeed all neo-Muslims were called by the generic but contemptuous term *julaha*. Surely all the converts could

1. *Loc. cit.*
2. Barani, *Fatawa-i-Jahandari*, p. 49.
3. *Ibid.*, p.98

not have come from the weaver caste, but the word *julaha* became synonymous with the despised low-born Indian Muslim convert.

On the other hand the foreign Muslims (or Turks) "alone are capable of virtue, kindness, generosity, valour, good deed, good works, truthfulness, keeping of promises...loyalty, clarity of vision, justice, equity, recognition of rights, gratitude for favours and fear of God. They are, consequently, said to be noble, free born, virtuous, religious, of high pedigree and pure birth. These groups, alone are worthy of offices and posts in the government.... Owing to their actions the government of the king is strenghened and adorned." On the other hand the "low-born" (Indian) Muslims are capable only of vices – immodesty, falsehood, miserliness, misappropriation, wrongfulness, lies, evil-speaking ingratitude,...shamlessness, impundence...So they are called low-born, bazaar people, base, mean, worthless, plebian, shameless and of dirty birth".[1] Now neither the one could be so good nor the other that bad, but Ziyauddin Barani rightly depicts the prevailing attitudes and consequent tensions. What worried him most was that the Indian Muslims were appointed to "high offices and are successful in their work...they will make people of their own kind their helpers, supporters, colleagues. They will not allow (Turkish) nobles and free-born men and men of merits to come anywhere near the affairs of the government."[2]

In short, there was a constant and bitter struggle of wit and influence for power going on between the "foreign" Turks and Indian Muslims – Indian Muslims both high and low. Although the claim of nobility of birth by purchased slaves makes little sense, the Turks felt that

1. *Loc. cit.*, p. 98.
2. Barani, *Fatawa-i-Jahandari*, pp. 97, 98, 99.

they belonged to blue blood and as founders of Muslim rule in India, they deserved special consideration. It was their right to keep to themselves all high offices, for they possessed merit and were superior to the *julahas*. The Indian Muslims knew that the Turks were good fighters, but for administrative work the indigenous Muslims were better suited if not indispensable. Muhammad bin Qasim and Mahmud Ghaznavi used to employ Hindus in administration and army. But with the permanent establishment of Muslim rule in India and the growth of Muslim population, the policy of the early sultans was to keep the Hindus excluded from offices and appoint only Muslims. Consequently, many ambitious Hindus converted to Islam to obtain offices. They were originally Brahmans or Kshatriyas or of other high classes and perhaps belonged originally to *raja, zamindar* or warrior families. Such converts had good chances of entering official positions because isolation from original homes and communities made them all the more reliable servants. They had intelligence and experience on account of their being sons of the soil. They carried with them their caste pride. In short, the Indian Muslim officers did not feel inferior to the Turks. While the poor sections of the neo-Muslims could bear any humiliation at the hands of the Turks, the higher class Indian Muslims hit back.

In this strife, the foreign Muslims had an edge. They were closer to the sultan and wielded influence with him. They were ever doing research on the ancestry of Indian Muslim officers, and informing the king about their origins and geneology with a view to denigrating them and attempting at the removal of those who had 'infiltrated' into it. Ziyauddin Barani derives a cynical pleasure in writing about the exclusion and expulsion of low-born Muslims from state employment. He says that Iltutmish dismissed thirtythree persons from government service by one stroke of the pen on account of their low birth. He also writes that the Vazir Nizamul Mulk Junaidi had appointed one Jamal Marzuq as the *Mutsarrif* (Superintendent) of Kannauj. The sultan not only cancelled the appointment of Marzuq, he even went into the antecedents of Nizamul Mulk himself on the representation of Malik Qutbuddin Hasan the Barbak and Malik Izzuddin Salari the Vali-i-Dar, who had some personal score to settle with the Vazir. Nizamul Mulk is highly praised by Muhammad Ufi, who dedicates his book the *Jami-ul-Hikayat* to the Vazir. This shows that he was high born. But it was not difficult for vested interests to prove that the Vazir's grandfather had descended from the *julaha* class. It is said that the latter lost the confidence of the sultan. But not his office. Obviously, the sultan dared not remove him. Barani wrongly writes that no Indian Muslim could be retained on an *iqta* or appointed to the post of *khwajgi, mutsarrifi* or *Mir Muharriri*. It is true that Balban also made detailed enquiries about the families of all his officers. He refused to grant audience to a low-born officer (*Amir-i-Bazariyan*) for "granting him an interview would reduce the status of the king in the eyes of the common people and diminish the prestige of the throne" [1] and removed one Kamal Maiyher from the *khwajgi* of Amroha. The situation never changed, and Francois Bernier, late in the seventeenth century, talks of originally "real Mongols", "White men, foreigners". He also says "that children of the third and fourth generation, who have the brown complexion... are held in much less respect than new comers, and are seldom invested with official situations: they consider themselves happy, if permitted to serve as private soldiers in the infantry or cavalry."[2]

1. For detailed reference see Lal, K.S., *Early Muslims in India* (New Delhi, 1984), pp.129-132.
2. Bernier, *Travels in the Mogul Empire*, p.209.

Chapter 3

Proselytization in Provincial Muslim Kingdoms

A year before the dawn of the fifteenth century, Timur had claimed to have invaded Hindustan to destroy its infidels and idolators.[1] In the year 1400 India was predominantly Hindu; Muslims comprised less than 2 per cent of the population. The country south of the Krishna River right up to Cape Camorin formed the Vijayanagar empire and it was Hindu. On the west coast, the strip between Goa in the south to Chaul and (future) Bombay in the north was in the hands of independent Hindu rulers. In the Bahmani kingdom conversions and immigration were swelling Muslim numbers. But the whole of Central India with Rajasthan to the west and Gondwana to the east was Hindu. East U.P., Bihar and Orissa were also Hindu. Only in Baluchistan, portion of the Punjab west of the River Ravi, Sind and Bengal there were good number of Muslims, but there too the Hindus were in majority. In the heart of the Sultanate – the eastern Punjab, Delhi and its outlying regions, and western U.P. – Gujarat, and Malwa, Muslim numbers were rising but were not yet large. Timur might have made his declaration merely as a champion of Islam, and yet he was not wrong in his assessment of the Hindu population of India.

After Timur's visitation, a number of independent Muslim-ruled kingdoms like Gujarat, Malwa, Khandesh and Jaunpur also came into being at the expense of the

---

1. Sharafuddin Yazdi, *Zafar Nama*, Bib. Ind. Text (Calcutta, 1885, 88), 2 vols., II, p.14. Also *Mulfuzat-i-Timuri*, trs. in E and D, II, p.429.

weakened Sultanate. Bahmani kingdom had declared independence about the middle of the fourteenth century, and Bengal too had become virtually independent. Curiously enough the break up of the Turkish empire hepled in the rapid rise of Muslim population in the fifteenth century. The Hindu rulers no doubt had gathered strength, but they had to keep on fighting against newly established Muslim kingdoms as well as the Delhi Sultanate and in the process, and whenever they were defeated, a number of their soldiers and subjects were captured and made Musalmans. Besides conversions of non-Muslims in India a large number of foreign Muslims also arrived from abroad during this period.

To keep themselves in power, the Saiyyad and Lodi Sultans of Delhi (1414-1526) went on inviting Afghans from beyond the Indus to help them stay in power. Consequently, a large number of Afghan leaders and men came into India like "ants and locusts" and helped in the rise of Muslim population.[1] All these factors helped in swelling the ranks of Muslims. In this context it is worth remembering that this period was, it appears, marked by feverish Muslim proselytization even outside India. All the European visitors to India like Nicolo Conti, Athnasius Nikitin and Santo Stefano were compelled to convert to Islam on their way to India.[2] In India itself, according to Barbosa, the sultans of Delhi had made life extremely difficult for the non-Muslims.[3] Many of the northern Hindus, especially the Yogis, "unwilling to stay under the power of the Moors", became wanderers.[4] Thus

1. So much so that Rizqullah says that under Sikandar Lodi one half of the country was assigned to the Farmulis and the other half to other Afghan tribes. *Waqiat-i-Mushtaqi*, trs. in E and D., IV, p.547.
2. Major, *India in the Fifteenth Century* (London, 1857) Introduction.
3. Barbosa, Duarte, *The Book of Durate Barbosa*, 2 Vols., (London, 1918-21), II, p.230.
4. *Ibid.*, I, 230-33.

like the fourteenth century, the fifteenth also was a century of rapid rise of Muslim numbers through immigration and conversion. In this chapter, therefore, we shall cursorily go through the history of these kingdoms of India which were ruled by Muslim kings, and see how Muslim number grew there in the fifteenth and sixteenth centuries.

The Sultanate – The Punjab, Sind and U.P.

During Timur's invasion the important places in the Punjab were systematically sacked. Punjab was always the first to bear the brunt of Muslim invasions directed against Hindustan, and Muslim invaders were keenly interested in making conversions. The Ghaznavids and Ghorids had occupied it and converted many people to Islam. The Mongols had also ravaged it occasionally. And for many years at a stretch, during the reigns of Sultan Nasiruddin and Ghayasuddin Balban (1246-86), they had held the trans-Ravi and Sind regions under their sway. Under them conversions used to take place on a large scale.[1] In the second quarter of the fifteenth century the successors of Timur were holding parts of the Punjab to ransom, and rebellions of Muslim adventures were creating anarchical conditions.[2] During this period and after, therefore, the Muslim population of the Punjab swelled considerably mainly due to proselytization. Immigration of foreign Muslims too was there on a good scale, for, as said earlier, the Saiyyad rulers, to deal effectively with foreign invaders and local rebles, and the Lodis to consolidate their position, invited large number of Afghans from across the Indus. Thus foreign immigration and campaigns helped in the rise of Muslim population in the fifteenth century Punjab.

---

1. Mohammad Habib, *Some Aspects of the Foundation of the Delhi Sultanate*, Dr. K.M. Ashraf Memorial Lecture (Delhi, 1966) p.20.
2. For the anarchical conditions in the Punjab see Lal, *Twilight*, pp.79-100.

Uttar Pradesh formed part of the Sultanate from its very inception. Consequently "its invasion", which brought converts, was ruled out. But in the fifteenth century, the region to the east and south of Delhi – Katehar, Doab, Bayana and Mewat – had become a problem tract under the Saiyyads, and there they contented themselves "with the ignoble but customary satisfaction of plundering the people",[1] and obtaining some converts in the bargain. In eastern U.P. the flourishing Muslim kingdom of Jaunpur again helped in the rise of Muslim numbers. However, the regular warfare between the Lodis and the Sharqis had made both of them loosen their grip on neighbouring Hindu Rajas and Zamindars. But when the Sultanate once again gathered stability, the policy of proselytization was revived with vigour. Sikandar Lodi is credited with sustained activity in this regard. His intolerance in Gwalior, Mathura, Banaras and Allahabad,[2] his various "Islamic" regulations, and the fact that a "contemporary (inscription) declares him a staunch Muslim who made the foundations of Islam strong",[3] point to large additions to Muslim demography.

By the fifteenth century Sind also contained a substantial population of Muslims, but when actually Sindhis converted to Islam in large numbers is not precisely known. However, Muslims had been growing in number there ever since the days of Mahmud of Ghazni. Like in Punjab, Ghaznavid governors had also ruled over upper Sind.[4] Later on the rule of Qubacha, his defeat by Iltutmish, the pressure of Mongols, and the rule of the Sultanate of Delhi had all combined to Islamize northern

---

1. *Ibid.*, pp.101-109. Also C.H.I. III, p.207.
2. Lal, *Twilight*, pp.77, 192.
3. *Ibid.*, p.187.
4. *Tuhfat-ul-Kiram*, E and D., I, pp.341-42.

Sind to a large extent. In southern Sind the Sumras, a native Rajput tribe, was ousted by another Rajput tribe, the Summas, in the fourteenth century. The Summas were Muslims and Hindus by turns,[1] but ultimately they seem to have "adopted Islam, and propagated the religion in their dominions,"[2] so that when Firoz Tughlaq invaded Tatta in 1361, he prohibited the plunder or captivity of the people because they were Muslims.[3] But the Hindus were also there in large numbers. When Sultan Mahmud Beghara of Gujarat received "complaints from Southern Sind where Muslims were said to be persecuted by Hindus," he marched to their relief in 1470. He met many leaders of Sumras, Sodas and Kalhoras who "told him that they were professing Muslims but knew little of their faith or its rules, and were wont to intermarry with and to live as Hindus." In Sind, "Compulsory conversions to Mahometanism were not infrequent, the helpless Hindu being forcibly subjected to circumcision on slight or misconstrued profession, or the false testimony of abandoned Mahometans."[4] Mahmud invited many of them to Gujarat "where teachers were appointed to instruct them in the faith of Islam."[5] In the first quarter of the sixteenth century, Shah Beg Arghun, driven from Qandhar by Babur, expelled Jam Firoz, the last of the Summas, and his son Shah Husain took Multan in 1528. When Humayun took refuge in Sind (1541)[6] Muslim population in the cities of Sind had grown considerably.

---

1. *Ibid.*, p.337.
2. C.H.I. III, p.501; also *Tarikh-i-Masumi*, E and D, I, pp. 224-26, and *Journal of the Asiatic Society of Bengal*, 1845, pp.159-60.
3. Afif, *op. cit.*, p. 233.
4. *Journal of the Asiatic Society of Bengal*, 1841, p.20. Even in the nineteenth century Hindus in the service of the Amir were obliged to wear beards like the Muslims. Thornton, *Gazetteer*, IV, p.296.
5. C.H.I., III, p.309.
6. *Ibid.*, pp. 501-502.

The countryside had a mixed population in which half-converted Muslims and Hindus predominated.

Kashmir

Kashmir's conversion to Islam on a large scale also dates from the beginning of the fifteenth century. Mahmud of Ghazni had made some stray efforts at preoselytization. Later on arrived in Kashmir one Shah Mirza in saintly robes from Swat in 1315. He entered the service of Sinha Deva, the ruling prince. Shah Mirza helped to oust the Hindu dynasty, and finally he himself ascended the throne in 1346.[1] Thus there were Muslim kings in the Kashmir Valley from the middle of the fourteenth century. However, it was during the reign of Sikandar Butshikan (1394-1417), that the wind of Muslim proselytization blew the strongest. He invited from Persia, Arabia and Mesopotamia learned men of his own faith; his bigotry prompted him to destroy all the most famous temples in Kashmir – Martand, Vishya, Isna, Chakrabhrit, Tripeshwar, etc. Sikandar offered the Kashmiris the choice between Islam and death. Some Kashmiri Brahmans committed suicide, many left the land, many others embraced Islam, and a few began to live under Taqiya, that is, they professed Islam only outwardly.[2] It is said that the fierce intolerance of Sikandar had left in Kashmir no more than eleven families of Brahmans.[3] His contemporary the Raja of Jammu had been converted to Islam by Timur, by "hopes, fears and threats".[4]

1. Ferishtah, II, p.337.
2. *Ibid.*, II, p.341.
3. C.H.I., III, p.281, Zain-ul-Abidin (1420-1470), the Akbar of Kashmir, recalled the exiles, assuaged the fears of the Hindus, and abolished the Jiziyah, but the converts continued to remain Musalman.
4. *Zafar Nama*, op. cit., II, pp.168-69. Lal, *Twilight*, p.39.

By the time of Akbar's annexation of Kashmir (C.E. 1586) the valley had turned mainly Mohammadan. When Father Xavier and Brother Benedict went to Kashmir with Akbar this is what they learnt: "In antiquity this land was inhabited by the Moors, possibly a reference to Timur (contemporary of Sikandar the Iconoclast), and since then the majority of the people accept Islam."[1]When Kashmir was under Muslim rule for 500 years (1319-1819) Hindus were constantly tortured and forcibly converted. A delegation of Kashmir Brahmans had approached Guru Teg Bahadur at Anandpur Saheb to seek his help.[2] But Kashmir was Islamized.

Those who fled to preserve their religion went to Laddakh in the east and Jammu in the south. It is for this reason that non-Muslims are found in large number in these regions. In the valley itself the Muslims formed the bulk of the population.

Gujarat

The kingdom of Gujarat was established in 1396 and its rulers were descended from Wajih-ul-Mulk, a converted Rajput. This dynasty made great efforts to spread Islam. One of its famous rulers, Ahmad Shah (1411-1442), was responsible for many conversions. In 1414 he introduced the Jiziyah, and collected it with such strictness, that it brought a number of converts to Islam.[3] This Jiziyah was not rescinded till Akbar's conquest of Gujarat in 1573. Even after that it took time to go,[4] bringing converts all the while. In 1420 Ahmad Shah punished

1. Lach, Donald F., *Asia in the Making of Europe*,(Chicago, 1965), vol.I, p.467.
2. Macauliffe, M.A. *The Sikh Religion*, 6 vols., IV, pp.371-72.
3. Ferishtah, II, pp. 184-185. Also Satish C. Misra, *The Rise of Muslim Power in Gujarat* (Bombay, 1963), p.175.
4. R.P. Tripathi, *Some Aspects of Muslim Administration* (Allahabad, 1936), p.318.

the 'infidels' of Satpura; in 1433 he raided Dungarpur and in 1440 he brought about Idar's submission.[1] All his conquests were accompanied by conversions and boosted Muslim demography. Mahmud Beghara's (1458-1511) exertions in the field of proselytization were equally impressive. In 1469 he led an army into Sorath against the Mandalik of Girnar. To the Raja's protests that he had paid the tribute regularly, Mahmud replied that he had come "neither for tribute nor for plunder, but to establish the true faith in Sorath." The Raja went on fighting and fleeing and resisting for a whole year, but then had to accept Islam,[2] and received the title of Khan-i-Jahan. It stands to reason that he did not convert alone. In 1473 a raid on Dwarka brought in some more converts. When Champaner was attacked, its Rajput Raja Patai fought very valiantly. He was defeated but refused to accept Islam. For this he was done to death with great barbarity.[3] In 1484 his son was made Musalman (again, not alone) and in the next reign became the Amir of Idar, receiving the title of Nizam-ul-Mulk.

About conversions through enslavement, Dr. Satish C. Misra, who has made a special study of the history of Gujarat, writes that "the conflict (in Gujarat) veered round two main objectives – land and women. The conqueror inexorably demanded, more often forcibly wrested, both land and women..."[4] Surely a large number of women would have been made Musalman during these wars.

Immigration of foreign Muslims was also not inconsiderable. Ferishtah writes that following the example of sultan Barbak Shah of Bengal, the sultans of Gujarat and the Deccan also invited groups of Abyssinians and gave

1. C.H.I., III, pp.298-300.
2. *Ibid.*, pp.305-06.
3. *Ibid.*, p.310. Ferishtah, II, p.202.
4. S.C. Misra, *op. cit.*, p.205.

them "positions of respect and trust."[1] But Gujarat needed no lessons from Bengal. She abounded in port-towns, and these were doing brisk trade. Her industry was also well-developed. Traders arrived from abroad as well as slaves and soldiers."Because of the constant threat from the Rajputs and other neighbouring peoples, the Sultan of Gujarat (maintained) a large standing army, recruited mostly from foreign Muslim adventurers to whom he (paid) handsome salaries." [2] On the basis of the writings of Barbosa, Cortesao and Azevedo, Professor Donald F. Lach summarises the situation thus: "Moors from all over the Islamic world congregate in the cities of Gujarat to carry on trade or to find employment as soldiers of the sultan. In addition to the native Moors and their co-religionists of Delhi, a cosmopolitan flavour is given to life by the presence of Turks, Mamlukes, Arabs, Persians, Khurasanis, Turcomans, Abyssinians, and a sprinkling of renegade Christians."[3]

In Cambay, Ratanpur and Rander, the Portuguese found a number of foreign and Indian Muslims.[4] According to Orta, who wrote around 1560, there were a few local Muslims and some low caste Hindus in Bassein when the Portuguese took it in 1535-36.[5]

Malwa

Since the days of Khalji and Tughlaq sultans of Delhi, there were large number of Muslims in Malwa, both indigenous and foreign.[6] These numbers went on

1. Ferishtah, II, p.298.
2. Castanheda, *Historia do descobrimento e conquista de India pelos Partugueses* (Third Ed. Coimbra, 1928), II, p.316. Mentioned in Lach, *Asia in the Making of Europe*, p. 399.
3. Lach, I, 401.
4. Barbosa, *op.cit.*, p.140; Orta and Pires in Lach, I, 404.
5. Lach, I, 405.
6. U.N. Day, *Medieval Malwa* (Delhi, 1967), pp.6-7.

growing during the rule of the independent Muslim rulers of Malwa, the Ghoris and Khaljis (1401-1562). The pattern of growth of Muslim population in Malwa was similar to that in the other regions. Captives made in campaigns against Kherla, Orissa, and Gagraun, in the first quarter of the fifteenth century, would have added to Muslim numbers. Similarly, when sultan Mahmud led an expedition against the Hara Rajputs in 1454, he put many of them to the sword, "and sent their children into slavery at Mandu."[1] In 1468 from the ravaged and burning town of Karahra (near Chanderi), 7,000 prisoners were taken.[2]

The harem of Malwa sultans formed a great source of proselytization. The seraglio of Ghayas-ud-din (1469-1500) was filled with beautiful slaves girls and daughters of Rajas and Zamindars.[3] The number of its inmates was 16,000 according to Nizamuddin and 10,000 according to Ferishtah.[4] However, with the rise of Rajputs to power in Malwa, the enslavement of Hindus and the proselytizing activity of Malwa rulers may not have been as sustained as in other regions. Foreign elements in the Malwa army and administration were also not conspicuous.

1. C.H.I., III p. 356.
2. *Ibid.*, p.360.
3. Day, *op.cit.*, p.244.
4. *Tabqat-i-Akbari*, III, p. 351. Ferishtah, II, 255. Dr. U.N. Day *op. cit.*, pp.244-46 thinks that the figure of Nizamuddin is exaggerated. Probably it is not. When it is realised that Ghayasuddin had two battalions of Habsh and Turkish women guards, each of 500, the figure of 1600 (given by Wolseley Haig) appears to be too small to be true. In fact according to Pires, who wrote between 1512 and 1515 the king of Malwa was said to have 2,000 women warriors who rode out to battle with him. (*The Suma Oriental of Tome Pires* (London,1944), I, p.37 cited in Lach, I, p.420). A harem of 1600 inmates would have hardly aroused any comment from medieval chroniclers. But Ghayas's saraglio was an unique institution. It was built with beauties collected from all over the world (Ferishtah). Girls were also abducted to supply its requirements. "Besides the musicians, singers, and dancers, usually found in a royal seraglio there were goldsmiths, blacksmiths, shoemakers, weavers, potters, tailors, makers of bows, arrows,

The Deccan

The Bahmani or the kingdom of the Deccan had come into being in 1347. With the extension of its dominion and power, Muslim population saw a rapid rise. Continual war with Vijayanagar, Orissa and other smaller Hindu kingdoms brought slaves who in course of time became Musalmans. Nobles and soldiers of foreign extraction filled the army and political life of the Deccan. A few instances of these would suffice to give an idea of the acceleration of Muslim numbers in the Deccan.

The first Bahmani king, Alauddin Bahman Shah (1347-1358) despatched an expedition against the northern Carnatic Hindu chieftains, and his booty included "1000 singing and dancing girls, *Murlis,* from Hindu temples."[1] In 1406 Sultan Tajuddin Firoz (1397-1422) fought a war with Vijayanagar and captured 60,000 youths and children from its territories. When peace was made Bukka gave, besides other things, 2,000 boys and girls skilled in dancing and music.[2] Incidentally Firoz had a harem of 800 women of various nations, but of course all Muslim.[3]

His successor Ahmad Vali (1422-36), marched through Vijayanagar kingdom, "slaughtering men and enslaving women and children."[4] The captives were made Musalmans.[5] Sultan Alauddin (1436-58) collected a thousand women in his harem. When it is noted that

---

and quivers, carpenters, wrestlers, and jugglers, each of whom received fixed wages, their officers, also women, being paid at high rates...". (W. Haig and Ferishtah). The wages – two seers of grain and two tankahs per head per day – given to harem inmates were so low as to make one feel that it was a stable for women rather than a harem. If the number was manageable the women would have been paid and looked after better. In view of all this, the figure of 16,000 may not, after all, be an exaggeration.

1. C.H.I., III p.375-76.
2. Sewell, *A Forgotten Empire (Vijayanagar)*, pp.57-58.
3. C.H.I., III, p. 391.
4. *Ibid.*, p.397.
5. *Ibid.*, p.398.

intermittent warfare between the Bahmani and Vijayanagar kingdoms continued for more than a century and a half, the story of enslavement, conversions, and harems of kings and nobles need not be carried on. Even ordinary soldiers used to get many slaves, and at the end of the battle of Talikot (1565), "large number of captives consigned to slavery, enriched the whole of the Muslim armies, for the troops were permitted to retain the whole of the plunder..."[1] Capture of women and children in wars with Telingana and southern chieftaincies too added to Muslim population.

The Deccan was also full of foreign Muslims. Most of Bahman Shah's nobles were foreigners. "His Afghan minister was succeeded by a Persian from Shiraz and he again by a native of Basrah."[2] Ahmad's son Alauddin also surrounded himself with foreigners. No wonder that in the Bahmani kingdom two parties sprang up – Foreigners (better termad as Afaqis) and Deccanis.[3] Both were at daggers drawn for power and in politics. Humayun (1458-61) bestowed his favours upon the Foreign faction. His renowned minister Mahmud Gawan was a foreigner, who kept an army of 20,000 men.[4] Another Malik-ul-Tujjar, the governor of Daulatabad, had with him 7,000 foreign horse.[5] Sultan Ahmad had a special corps of 3,000 archers from Iraq, Khurasan Transoxiana, Turkey and Arabia.[6]

There were thus foreigners of all extractions in the Deccan – Arabs, Afghans, Abyssinians, Egyptians, Persians and Turks. Names of some officers like Saiyyad Husain Badakhshi, Mir Ali Sistani, Abdulla Kurd, Qara

1. *Ibid.*, III, 449. Also Sewell, p.198.
2. *Ibid.*, III, pp.403-404.
3. H.K. Sherwani, *Mahmud Gawan* (Allahabad, 1942), pp. 61-71, esp. p.63 and n.50.
4. C.H.I., III, p.432.
5. *Ibid.*, p.406.
6. Sherwani, *op. cit.*, p.65.

Khan Kurd, Ali Khan Sistani and Iftakhar-ul-Mulk Hamadani are indicative of their foreign extration and predominant position.[1] Besides the Bahmani kingdom, Vijayanagar also employed a large number of Muslims in its armies.

One class of foreigners, the Africans, need special mention. Their dark skin made them a class apart, not being considered equal by the other fair-skinned foreigners. "To the negroes were added the *Muwallads*, a name applied to African fathers and Indian mothers."[2] In politics they were partisans of the Deccanis, in status "low caste", in number very large. It would not be unsafe to assume that at the end of the fifteenth century foreigners in the Deccan were in the neighbourhood of a million.

The Malabar Coast

In Malabar, Muslim population increased considerably during the period of fourteenth-fifteenth-sixteenth centuries. In Quilon, the pearl fishery was monopolized by the Muslims who were there in large numbers. Such was their strength and influence that, although the ruler of Quilon and his armed retainers were always close by the city, the real arbiters of justice in local affairs seemed to be the wealthy "Moors" who ran the fishery.[3] Both Barbosa and Barros talk of the large number of Muhammadans, both foreign and indigenous, in Malabar. The foreigners included Arabs, Persians, Gujaratis, Khurasanis and Deccanis. The local ones were called Moplahs. They were mostly Sunnis, they lived in cities and made their living by trade. They comprised about 20 per cent of the total population.[4] Barbosa contends that they were so

1. *Ibid.*, pp.65-68.
2. C.H.I., III, p.404.
3. Barbosa, II, pp. 122-23.
4. W. Logan, *Malabar* (Madras, 1951), I, p.199. Also Lach,368-69. On the impression of Barbosa and Barros.

numerous that the advent of the Portuguese alone prevented Malabar from becoming "a Moorish state."[1] A letter from Goa of the Year 1568 asserts that "the Malabar nation is Muslim, and they are almost all pirates and hostile to the Christians."[2] But the arrival of the Portuguese provided a check and a challenge to Muslim proselytizing endeavour. They had captured Goa, Daman and Diu in the early years of the sixteenth century. In their triumphal entry into Goa (C.E. 1510), "the clergymen were at the head of the procession." Albuquerque encouraged his soldiers to marry in the families of his Turkish officers. Force was also openly used for obtaining converts. And we shall see later on, the Portuguese tried to check conversion to Islam.

Bengal

Sind and Punjab lay on the route of Muslim invaders. They bore the brunt of so many Muslim invasions for a thousand years from 712 to 1761. In these provinces as well as North West Frontier Province and Baluchistan Muslim immigration too was considerable. Therefore, the extensive growth of Muslim population in this region is understandable. But Bengal, especially eastern Bengal, calls for a special study, for Bengal did not lie on the route of the Muslim invaders. Nor did it form a base of operations for further conquests into India as were Punjab and Sind. But Bengal was another region where the rise of Muslim population was rapid, and probably in the medieval period itself eastern Bengal especially began to have a majority of Muslim population. An explanation for this phenomenon has posed a problem before scholars and demographers. However, as we shall

3. Barbosa, II, p.74.
4. Lach, *op. cit.*, I, p. 447.

see presently, the overall picture of Islamization in Bengal is quite clear: only in details it is a little blurred.

The main reasón for large-scale conversions in Bengal, as indeed elsewhere, lies in the proselytizing endeavour of its Muslim rulers and (this is peculiar to Bengal) Sufi Mashaikh. Muslim invasions from northern India had started from the early years of the thirteenth century. Bakhtiyar Khalji had invaded Nadia (1203) and Balban had marched (c. 1279-80) as far as Sonargaon in eastern Bengal. The Tughlaqs continued to assert their authority over Bengal and led many expeditions into it. During such campaigns some usual conversions would have taken place. But large number of Muslims were made under the independent Muslim rulers of Bengal. "It is evident, from the numerical superiority in Eastern Bengal of the Muslims...that at some period an immense wave of proselytization must have swept over the country and it is most probable that that period was the period of Jalaluddin Muhammad (converted son of Hindu Raja Ganesh) during whose reign of seventeen years (1414-1431)...hosts of Hindus are said to have been forcibly converted to Islam."[1] About these Dr. Wise writes that "the only condition he offered were the Koran or death...many Hindus fled to Kamrup and the jungles of Assam, but it is nevertheless probable that more Muhammadans were added to Islam during these seventeen years (1414-31) than in the next three hundred."[2]

Employment prospects also helped in the rise of Muslim population, for says Barbosa: "It is obviously an advantage in the sixteenth century Bengal to be a Moor, in as much as the Hindus daily become Moors to gain the favour of their rulers."[3]

1. C.H.I., III, p.267.
2. *Journal of the Asiatic Society of Bengal,* 1894, Pt. III, p.28.
3. Barbosa, *The Book of Duarte Barbosa,* II, p.148. Also Castanheda cited in Lach, I, p. 415.

Moreover, "the enthusiastic soldiers, who, in the thirteenth and fourteenth centuries, spread the faith of Islam among the timid race of Bengal, made forcible conversions by the sword, and, penetrating the dense forests of the Eastern frontier, planted the crescent in the villages of Sylhet. Tradition still preserves the names of Adam Shahid, Shah Halal Mujarrad, and Karmfarma Sahib, as three of the most successful of these enthusiasts."[1] The story of conversions under independent Muslim kings of Bengal (1338-1576) is not very clear as written records about them are few, but stray references clearly show that "at some times and in some places, the Hindus were subjected to persecution."[2] Tradition creedits the renowned Shah Jalal of Sylhet making large-scale conversions. In Mardaran thana in Arambagh sub-division of Hoogly, where the Muhammadan population predominates over the Hindu, there is a tradition that Muhammad Ismail Shah Ghazi defeated the local Hindu Raja and forcibly converted the people to Islam.[3]

Hand in hand with the proselytizing efforts of the rulers was the work of Sufis and Maulvis. From the time of Muhammad bin Tughlaq to that of Akbar, Bengal had attracted rebels, refugees, Sufi Mashaikh, disgruntled nobles and adventurers from northern India. The militant type of Mashaikh found in Bengal a soil fertile for conversion, and worked hard to raise Muslim numbers. Professor K.R. Qanungo has noted that the conversion of Bengal was mainly the work of Barah-Auliyas.[4] Professor Abdul Karim has also referred to militant Sufi proselytization.[5]

1. *Loc. cit.*
2. *Census of India Report*, 1901. VI, Pt. I, Bengal, pp. 165-181.
3. *Ibid.*
4. "Bengal was not conquered by seventeen Turkish cavalieres (of Bakhtiyar Khalji); but by the *barah-auliyas*, or twelve legendary Muslim militant saints, the Pirs who cropped up after the seed of Islam had been broadcast in the plains of Bengal." K.R. Qanungo, *op. cit.*, p. 151.
5. Abdul Karim, *Social History of Muslims in Bengal*, pp.136-38, 143-146.

But Dr. I.H. Qureshi is the most explicit in this regard. He writes: "The fourteenth century was a period of expansion of Muslim authority in Bengal and the adjoining territories. A significant part was played in this process by the warrior saints who were eager to take up the cause of any persecuted community. This often resulted (in clash) with the native authority, followed, almost invariably, by annexation..."[1] This also shows how elastic were the methods adopted by the Sufis. They acted mostly as peaceful missionaries, but if they saw that the espousal of some just cause required military action, they were not averse to fighting. "The Sufis...did not adopt the Ismaili technique of gradual conversion...They established their *khanqahs* and shrines at places which had already had a reputation for sanctity before Islam. Thus some of the traditional i.e. (Hindu) gatherings were transformed into new festivals. (i.e. Muslim). As a result of these efforts, Bengal in course of time became a Muslim land..."[2] In brief, the Sufi Mashaikh converted people by both violent and non-violent means,occupied their places of worship and turned them into *khanqahs* and mosques to make Eastern Bengal specially a Muslim land.

Stories of forcible conversions in Bengal are narrated by Muhammadan medieval historians themselves with great gusto and we need not dilate upon them.[3] From early times "each seat of Government, and

1. On the authority of Jadunath Sarkar, *History of Bengal*, pp.68, 70.
2. Ishtiaq Husain Qureshi, *The Muslim Community of the Indo-Pakistan Subcontinent* (610-1947), Monton & Co., 'S–Gravenhage, 1962, pp.70-71, 74-75.
3. Here is one such story cited in the Census of India Report, 1901, Vol. VI, Pt, I, Bengal, pp.165-181.

"While the Muhammadan population was still scattered, it was customary for each householder to hang an earthen water-pot (*badana*) from his thatched roof, as a sign of his religious belief. One day a Maulvi, after some years' absence, went to visit a disciple, who lived in the centre of a Hindu village, but could not find the 'badana'. On enquiry he was told

each military station was more or less a centre of missionary agitation". We find another agency from across the seas working towards the same end. Arab merchants carried on an extensive and lucrative trade at Chittagong and disseminated their religious ideas among its inhabitants. When Barbosa visited Bengal at the beginning of the sixteenth century, he found the inhabitants of the interior Gentiles, subject to the king of Bengal who was a Moor, while the sea ports were inhabited by both Moors and Gentiles. He also met with many foreigners – Arabs Persians, Abyssinians and Indians (probably Gujaratis). Caesar Frederick and Vincent Le Blanc, who were in Bengal in 1570, also inform us that the island of Sandip was then inhabited by Moors.[1] In the fifteenth and sixteenth centuries Chittagong surely was one of the centres from which unceasing propagandism was carried on. When it is realised how Muslim merchants from India played a major role in the conversion of Mallaca and then the other parts of South-East Asia to Islam,[2] an appreciation of their proselytizing endeavour and achievements in Gujarat, Malabar and Bengal can be easily made. Thus foreign Muslims were there too in large numbers in Bengal. They migrated on several occasions and for various reasons. Some came in the wake of conquest, others as traders and businessmen.[3] Ruknuddin

---

that the Musalman villager had renounced his faith and joined an outcaste tribe. On his return to the city, the circumstances being reported to the Nawab, a detachment of troops was ordered out, the village surrounded, and every person in it compelled to become Muhammadan."

Also see M.L. Roy Chowdhury, "Preaching of Islam in Bengal (Turko-Afghan Period)", in *Proceedings of the Indian History Congress,* Twentythird Session, Aligarh, 1960, Pt. I, pp.168-181, esp. p.171, where quotations from Bijoygupta's *Padma-Purana* and Jayananda's *Chaitanaya Mangal* show some methods of forcible conversions.

1. *Voyages de Le Goowz,* p.157, cited in Census Report, 1901, *op. cit.*
2. D.G.E. Hall, *A History of South East Asia,* pp.177-183.
3. Abdul Karim, p.140-41.

Barbak Shah (1460-74) was probably the first ruler who maintained a large number of Abyssinians as protectors of his throne. He recruited 8,000 Habshis and gave them key positions in his government. Aside from the Abyssinian eunuchs at the court, it was common for other eunuchs to act as harem guards.[1] In addition to the Abyssinians, Bengal played host to other foreigners, especially merchants from Arabia, Egypt, Turkey and other parts of India. Many stayed on in Bengal because of its fertility, riches and cheap food.[2] "Little is reported by European writers about the Hindu population of Bengal beyond remarks to the effect that their children are sometimes sold to be eunuchs, that many of them become converts to the Muslim faith, and that they constitute the majority of the population outside the port cities."[3] While European accounts of Gaur talk of a mixed population of Muslims, Hindus and foreigners (Moors), the *Manasa Vijaya* of Vipradasa (composed 1495) mentions large population of Muslims in Satgaon. It says, "The Muslim population of Saptagrama is innumerable; they belong to the Mughals, Pathans and Mokadims, Saiyyads, Mullas and Qazis...."[4] Obviously Bengal cities had a good number of Muslims in the fifteenth and sixteenth centuries.

The methods of conversion employed in Bengal were the same as seen elsewhere in medieval India. But what made Bengal different from many other parts of India as nonresistant and vulnerable to conversions was its peculiar political, religious, and social condition. Politically, Bengal could not withstand Muslim attacks from the very beginning as is clear from the shocking non-resistance of Lakshman Sen to Bakhtiyar Khalji's invasion.

1. Barbosa, II,147.
2. Lach, I, 416
3. *Ibid.*, I, pp.417-18.
4. Sukumar Sen, *Bangla Sahityer Itihasa* (Calcutta,1940), p.114, cited in Abdul Karim, *op. cit.*, p.153.

Perhaps the kingdom was already thoroughly infiltrated by Muslim adventures from the west and traders from the north. Its Muslim governors and rulers, due to its geographical location and the unsatisfactory medieval means of communication, mostly remained independent of Delhi, provoking, nevertheless, occasional attacks from the Delhi Sultans. Such emergencies brought the local rulers and the people closer to each other. Besides, "throughout the period from the 13th to the 18th century, the northern, eastern and south-eastern frontiers of the Muslim ruled area of East Bengal remained in fluid condition and the boundaries swung to and fro with tides of fresh conquests..."[1] (and conversions).

Thus the People of Bengal accepted their Muslim rulers as one of themselves, and the rulers on their part adopted and patronised the people's language and literature, art and culture.[2] Translations of many important Hindu works were done at the orders of Muslim rulers,[3] and "as a result of this interaction of Hinduism and Islam curious syncretic cults and practices arose, (there) grew the worship of a common God, adored by Hindus and Muslims alike, namely, Satya Pir. The Emperor Hussain Shah of Gauda is supposed to be the originator of this cult..."[4] Adherents of such cults provided potential converts to Islam. Muslim rulers were keen on increasing Muslim numbers. They could provide jobs and other economic incentives to conversions and, as has been pointed out earlier, Barbosa was struck by the fact that in Bengal "everyday Gentiles turn Moors to obtain favour of the King and Governors". Others converted as the only

1. Nafis Ahmad, "The Evaluation of the Boundaries of East Pakistan" in the *Oriental Geographer*, II, No. 2, July, 1958, p.101.
2. D.C.Sen, *History of Bengali Language and Literature* (Calcutta University, 1911), pp.10, 12, 13-14.
3. Tara Chand, *op. cit.*, p.214.
4. *Ibid.*, p.217.

means of escaping punishment for crimes. Besides, wherever Muhammadan rule existed slavery was developed, and "slavery was accepted by the Hindus as a refuge for their troubles. Delhi court obtained not only its slaves (in thousands, as for example under Firoz Tughlaq) but also eunuchs from the villages of Eastern Bengal (a wide-spread practice which the Mughal Emperor Jahangir tried to stop). The incursions of Assamese Maghs, the famines, pestilences and civil wars...drove them in sheer desperation to sell their children as Musalman slaves".[1]

To such compulsions obviously the very poor and socially backward people would have succumbed. For the rich other methods were brought into operation. The Census of India Report of 1901 says that "the tyrannical Murshid Kuli Khan enforced a law that any Amal, or Zamindar, failing to pay the revenue that was due...should, with his wife and children, be compelled to become Muhammadans", but the practice was much older as vouched by the *Banshasmriti*.[2] Conversions, such as that

1. Census of India Report, *op. cit.*, for 1901.

2. It gives a historical sketch and geneology of the family of Raja of Samudragarh, a place situated between Katwa and Bandel Railway Stations. Since the writer Satya Krishna Biswas was descended from Gopi Mohan Biswas, the last Diwan of the ruling house (*op. cit.*, p.10), the narrative appears to be quite reliable. It says that after Bakhtiyar Khalji overran Bengal, it became a rule that if revenue was not deposited within the prescribed time, the defaulting landlord (*bhuswami*) had either to lose his land or become Muslim. This is also referred to in the *Banglar Itihasa* of Babu Raj Krishna (p.7). *Banshasmriti* says that once Raja Ranjit Bhatt of Samudragarh went to deposit his land revenue, but at the Treasury he found that the Raja of Krishnanagar had not reached in time. He reflected that if the Raja of Krishnanagar became Muslim, much harm would be done because he was a bigger landlord. Therefore, "in the larger interest of Hinduism", Ranjit Bhatt deposited his money as revenue on behalf of the Raja of Krishnanagar and himself became a Muslim. But the most interesting part of the narrative is that on his return to his land the newly converted Raja started compelling others also to embrace Islam (because perhaps therein alone lay his security and defence).

of the Raja of Samudragarh, had a chain reaction. The converted Rajas and Zamindars used to compel others in their lands to become Musalmans for fear of losing their support, nay even for making them their active Muslim supporters. In this regard we have seen the achievements of Sultan Jalaluddin, himself a convert form Hinduism. Kala Pahar, the dreaded iconoclast, and Murshid Quli Khan were Brahman converts. So was Pir Ali or Muhammad Tahir, a Brahman apostate, who "like all renegades...probably proved a worse persecutor of his original faith than others who were Muhammadans by birth." The Census report of 1901 continues to say: "The present Raja of Parsouni in Darbhanga is descended form Raja Pudil Singh, who rebelled against the Emperor and became a Muhammadan by way of expiation. The family of Asad Khan of Baranthan in Chittagong, has descended from Syam Rai Chowdhari who was fain to become a Musalman...The Diwan families of Pargana Sarail in Tippera, and of Haibatnagar and Jangalbari in Mymensingh, the Pathans of Majhauli in Darbhangha", all sprang from old Hindu houses. They, their propagation, and their progeny added to Muslim numbers.

The religious condition of Bengal too made people vulnerable to Muslim proselytization. The Pala rulers of Bengal were Buddhists and Buddhism, in spite of the damage caused to it by Bakhtiyar Khalji, remained prevalent in the land until at least the fourteenth century. The Senas were Hindus. They patronised Brahmins and Sanskrit. They were destroyed by Bakhtiyar, but not

---

According to the author of the *Banshasmriti* the family still lives in Samudragarh, now only a small village. All the members are given two names – one Hindu and the other Muslim at the namakaran ceremony. The present Raja's (1926?) Muslim name is Ichamat Khan and HIndu name is Makhan Lal Thakur.

Hinduism.[1] However, a sort of rivalry between Buddhism and Hinduism,[2] and zeal of Muslim "Saints" combined to create a situation for people's exposure to conversion.

The social structure of Bengal too was not coalesced . It was an amalgamation of Hindus, non-Hindus, and foreigners. The invaders and immigrants from the side of Assam, Tibet and Burma were not Hindus. Abdul Majid Khan even goes on to say: "In fact India or the land of the Hindus ended in Bengal west of the Bhagirathi."[3] The statement is not quite true, but in the Bengal Census Report of 1872 Beverley has explained in great detail the difficulty of settling who are and who are not Hindus.[4] The dark, short and broadnosed people of Bengal are called pre-Dravidian by anthropologists. Tibeto-Chinese or Mongoloids also came into Bengal and have become part and parcel of the people. It is not known when the Bodo section of the Tibeto-Burman branch of these people (Bodo, Mech, Koch, Kachari, Rabha, Garo, Tipra) came to Assam and East Bengal, but are found spread all over North and East Bengal.

In brief in eastern Bengal, Chandals and Pods and in northern Rajbansis and Koches predominated; the proportion of orthodox Hindus was very small. Pods, Chandals and Koches all have traces of Buddhist influence. Among Koches traces of Buddhist influence still survived when Ralph Fitch visited the country in the sixteenth century.[5] Muslim religion must have crumbled the defences of Chandals, Koches, Pods and other tribes

1. P. Saran, *Resistance of Indian Princes to Turkish Offensive*, Sita Ram Kohli Memorial Lectures, Punjabi University (Patiala, 1967), p.34.
2. R.C. Mitra, *The Decline of Buddhism in India*, pp.78-79.
3. Abdul Majid Khan, "Research about Muslim Aristocracy in East Pakistan" in Pierre Bessaignet (Editor), *Social Research in East Pakistan*, pp.18-25.
4. p.131, also pp.96, 129.
5. *Journal of the Asiatic Society of Bengal*, 1873, Pt. I, p.240.

and low classes on whom there was little Hindu influence. Thus it were the peculiar political, religious, but more especially social conditions of Bengal that exposed its people much more to Muslim proselytization. Had the common, poor, unsophisticated sections of the backward classes been left to themselves, they might have remained contented with their local forms of devotion and folk culture. But Muslim rulers, soldiers and Sufi Mashaikh left the high and the low hardly any choice in the matter. The lower classes of course were more vulnerable. However, the picture of proselytization in Bengal is not very clear and the problem is still open to study.

But there can be no doubt as to the local origin of most of the Muhammadans in Bengal, especially in North and East. Dewan Fazle Rabbi, however, has tried to prove that Bengal Muslims are mainly of foreign extraction. Nothing can be farther from the truth, but before we critically assess his ill-founded thesis, we shall sift the evidence about the local origin of Bengal Muslims which in itself would refute their extra-Indian nativity. Brian Hodgson writes about the voluntary conversion of Koch tribe of North Bengal,[1] Dr. Wise about the tribes about Dacca, and Buchanan Hamilton about other tribes, but they all agree that Bengal Muslims are descendants of local inhabitants.[2] And the appellations and professions of the low class indigenous people did not change with their conversion, as will be clearly seen in the following Table.

1. *Essays on Indian Subjects*, I, p.108, cited in Census of India Report, VI, Pt.I

2. *Statistical Account of Rangpur*, p.221, cited in Census Report, 1901, VI, Pt. I, Bengal, pp.165-181.

Table
Showing Muslim Functional Castes in Eastern Bengal[1]

Name of the Group	Where reported	Traditional occupation
Badiya or Abdul	Bogra	Circumcisers
Bajadars	Jessore	Musicians
Chunia	Bogra	---
Dai	Dacca, etc.	Women act as midwives
Dhawa	Bogra and Rajshahi	Fishermen
Duffadi	Malda	Hooka sellers
Karindi	Jessore	Originally hawkers of glass beads, now engaged in agricultural operations.
Kathara	Bogra	Originally workers in lead foil used to decorate image of Durga, now gold and silver workers.
Kulu	Bogra, etc.	Oilpressers
Kutti	Dacca	Masons, hackney-carriage drivers, etc.
Mahifarash	Dacca	Fishermen

1. Extract from *Census of India*, 1931, V, Part I, p.423.

Manjhi	Bogra	Fishermen and boatmen, now turning to agriculture.
Mirshikari	Bogra and Dacca	Now goldsmiths
Naliya	Bogra	Weavers of reed mats
Pirkhodali	Malda	---
Punjhra	Malda	Fish sellers
Rasua	Jessore	Hawkers of glass-ware
Sanaidar	Dacca	Drummers
Sandar	Bogra	Hawkers of glass bangles and tinsel.

In other parts of the old province of Bengal also the general opinion, buttressed by census enumerations, is that the Muhammadans are recruited mainly from local converts.

It may be generally said that almost the whole of the functional groups such as Julaha and Dhunia and the great majority of Shaikhs, probably nine-tenths in Bengal and possibly half in Bihar, are of Indian origin. The foreign elements may be looked for chiefly in the ranks of the Saiyyads, Pathans and Mughals. Even here there are many who are descended from Hindus, because high caste converts are often allowed to assume high titles. "In Bihar a converted Hindu of the Brahman or Kayasth caste is usually allowed to call himself a Shekh (Shaikh) and to associate and intermarry with genuine Shekhs. A Babhan or Rajput in the same circumstances, becomes a Pathan....In Mymensingh high caste converts are given title of Khan and call themselves Pathans...(Even) the lower castes... after the lapse of some years... are gradually recognised as Shekh."[1] As Nazmul Karim rightly points out: "The pseudo-Syeds have been on the increase not only in India but thoroughout the Muslim world, even from the beginning of Islamic history",[2] and the high titles among Bengal Muslim do not nesessarily point to their foreign extraction.

Khan Bahadur Dewan Fazle Rabbi of Murshidabad wrote a book in Urdu entitled *Haqiqat-i-Musalman-i-Bangala*[3] to prove that Bengal Muslims were mainly of foreign extraction. This was done probably to controvert the statement of Beverley in the Census Report of 1872 that "the existence of Muhammadans is due not so much to the introduction of the Moghal blood into the country, as to the conversion of the former inhabitants." Mr. Abu Ghaznavi of Mymensingh, who prepared an excellent account of the Muhammadans of his district, probably in connection with the 1901 census, also supported the foreign origin theory, but he admitted that local converts bulked largely in the total. In Muhammadan histories no mention is made of any large-scale Muhammadan immigration from Upper India, and in Akbar's time the climate of Bengal was considered so uncongenial that an order to proceed there was considered a punishment. Muslims came to Bihar first, but there their number has remained small. Foreign Muslims would not have chosen to settle in the swampy regions of Noakhali, Bogra and Backergunje.

1. *Census of India Report*, 1901, VI, Part I, Bengal, pp.165-181.
2. A.K. Nazmul Karim, "Muslim Social Classes of East Pakistan" in *Changing Society in India and Pakistan*, University of Dacca (Oxford University Press, Pakistan, 1956), pp.120-30, 138-143.
Karim also quotes the well-known saying '*Pesh az yin qassab budem, badazan gushtem shiekh: ghalla chun arzan shawad, imsal syed meshawem.*"
(The first year we were butchers, the next Sheikhs, this year, if prices rise, we shall become Syeds).
3. Its English translation is also available, entitled *The Origin of the Muhammadans of Bengal*, Thacker, Spink & co., Calcutta, 1895.

In short, analysing the data collected by Mahalanobis in 1945 about the ethnic groups of eastern Bengal mainly, Majumdar and Rao also arrived at the conclusion that Muslims of Bengal are of indigenous origin mainly from lower classes.[1] These accepted Islam with their local prejudices, minor beliefs, forms of devotion, folk tales and folk cultures, and of course retaining Bengali as their mother tongue. And this explains the great rise of Muslim population in Bengal which did not lie on the route of Muslim invaders and was also situated far away from the seat of Muslim imperial power.

In conclusion it may be emphasised that even when historical forces had divided the country into a number of independent states consequent on the break-up of the Delhi Sultanate, the work of proselytization continued unabated. Indeed, it made the task of conversion easy. Small regions could be dealt with in detail and severe Muslim rulers, orthodox Ulema and zealous Sufis worked in them effectively. It was due to extraordinary situations that the Kashmir valley and Eastern Bengal became Muslim-majority regions as far back as the fifteenth century. In other parts of the country, where there was a Muslim ruler, Muslim population grew apace in the normal and usual way.

1. D.N.Majumdar and C.R. Rao, *Race Elements in Bengal,* Asia Publishing House (Bombay, 1960), pp. 74-77.

Chapter 4

Growth under the Mughals

By the time Akbar the Great (1556-1605) embarked upon the policy of reuniting these kingdom under his imperial banner, Muslim population was rising all over the country. Still, despite all the exertion of the Muslims at proselytization, Hindu resistance to it was also admirably effective. Sind and Punjab no doubt had a sizeable Muslim population. But at the beginning of the sixteenth century, northern Sind (north of the River Indus) had, according to Portuguese accounts, a local Hindu as its ruler or governor.[1] In Gujarat, Malwa, and Khandesh Muslims were growing in numbers ever since Alauddin Khalji had conquered these kingdoms, but mostly in the cities and seaports. In the interior the Hindus predominated. However, the notices of some foreigners show that Muslim population in Gujarat had risen considerably. The people of Cambay were both Moors and Hindus, wrote Barbosa.[2] and according to the impression of Pires, the Hindus had been reduced to "almost the third part of the kingdom."[3] On the Malabar coast, according to Portuguese estimates, the Muslims comprised about twenty percent of the population.[4] The Bahmani kingdom had a large number of Muslims which went on growing with time. In Ahmadnagar, Bijapur, Golkunda, Bidar, and Berar, the

---

1. Lach, I, p.420, referring to the authority of Pires.
2. Barbosa, *op. cit.*, I, p.40.
3. Pires, *op. cit.*, cited in Lach, I, p.390.
4. Lach, *op. cit.*, I, pp.368-69.

successor kingdoms of Bahmani, large number of foreign Muslims swelled the ranks of the indigenous. Writing on April, 7, 1561, C. Rodrigues remarks that in Bijapur "the Moors are as innumerable as insects."[1] Another region to which this epithet could be applied was Bengal. Even so the Muslims were not in a majority even in these parts. In the Vijayanagar empire there were a few Muslim contingents of soldiers and some Muslim citizens, but south of the river Krishna the Muslim numbers were microscopic. In the rest of the country Hindu population predominated. The Haryana, Delhi, Agra, and western U.P. regions formed the nucleus, first of the Sultanate of Delhi and then of the Mughal Empire. It was no enemy territory where warfare for conquest would have brought converts; its revenues in kind fed the capital cities of Delhi and Agra; and its aggressive Zamindars were left in restrained peace. Consequently this region remained largely Hindu. Here the small minority of Muslims was introduced as a result of early Turkish victories and Muslim immigrants were added largely under the Saiyyads and Lodis. Rajputana was Hindu; Muslims there were in insignificant numbers, because there Muslim rule could never get a foothold. Indeed when Father Pinheiro and his caravan were going from Cambay to Akbar's court at Lahore through Ahmedabad, Patan and Rajasthan,[2] in the course of the journey they passed through numerous large cities which were devastated, "especially the mosques therein."[3] In the east, according to Fitch, Banaras was a great city peopled exclusively by Hindus.[4] He also says that the inhabitants of Kuch Bihar were entirely

1 Lach, I, p.444.

2. Smith, *Akbar the Great Mogul*, p.188.

3. Peruschi in Lach, I, p.462.

4. Richard Hakluyt, *The Principal Navigations, Voyages, Traffiques, and Discovries of the English Nation* (Glasgow, 1903-05), V, p.477.

Hindu.[1] The vast majority of the population of Orissa too was Hindu; and Muslims were very few.[2] Similar was the case with Gondwana and Central India.

About the percentage of Muslims in the total population no precise information can be obtained from the contemporary records. Babur's statement that most of the inhabitants were Hindus, conveys only a general impression. Two facts are, however, certain. First, it is widely recognised that the majority of Muslims were converts from Hinduism. Secondly, the largest number of conversions took place under the Turks and Afghans who ruled between C. 1300 and 1556.

There is one contemporary source which gives precise information about the proportion of Muslims in the total population, but it is not reliable. The *Tarikh-i-Salim Shahi*, [3] an autobiographical memoir of Jahangir, mentions that on one occasion he inquired from his father why all inhabitants of India could not be made Musalmans, and Akbar is reported to have said: "My dear child... with all of God's creatures, I am at peace; why should I permit myself, under any consideration, to be the cause of molestation or aggression to any one? Besides, are not five parts in six of mankind either Hindus or aliens to the faith; and were I to be governed by motives of the kind

1. Lach, I, p.481.
2. Barbosa, *op. cit.*, II, pp.132-33.
3. "Memoirs of the Emperor Jahangueir, written by himself, and translated from a Persian Manuscript" by Major David Price (London, 1829), p.15. Calcutta Edition (Bangabasi Press, 1906), pp.21-22.
This work, according to Sir Henry Elliot, does not comprise the real *Tuzuk-i-Jahangiri* or *Memoirs of Jahangir*. He also points out a number of exaggerations in which the *Tarikh-i-Salim Shahi* indulges (E and D, VI, pp. 256-264), and adds that "some parts at least...must be ranked in the same class" as fiction. (E and D, VI, p.257).
Dr. Beni Prasad, writing on the *Tarkikh-i-Salim Shahi* says: "The name of the author is unknown. On several points it is fuller than the genuine memoirs. But the work as a whole is a fabrication." *History of Jahangir*, pp. 387-88.

suggested in your inquiry, what alternative can I have but to put them all to death? I have thought it therefore my wisest plan to let these men alone."[1]

Jahangir is supposed to have repeated this ratio at another place. "Of the whole population of Hindustan it is notorious that five parts in six are composed of Hindus, the adorers of images, and the whole concerns of trade and manufacture... are entirely under the management of these classes. Were it, therefore, ever so much my desire to convert them to the true faith, it would be impossible, otherwise than through excision of millions of men... but the massacre of a whole people can never be any business of mine."[2]

These statements, attributed to Jahangir, about the proportion of Muslim population could not have been easily brushed aside but for the fact that they appear to be obviously wrong. From what we know of Akbar and Jahangir, such sentiments and statements cannot be attributed to them. Whosoever be the writer of the *Tarikh-i-Salim Shahi,* he cannot delude us because, as will be seen later, Muslims were not one-sixth of the Hindu population even as late as the year 1800. By 1600 Muslim numbers may not have risen beyond 15 million. In that year the total population of India has been estimated at 140 millions. Muslims would have formed about one-ninth to one-tenth of India's total population.[3]

During the first quarter of the seventeenth century, Jahangir, by and large, continued to follow Akbar's policy of *sulehkul.* Perhaps a few cases of forcible conversions might have been brought to his notice so as to prompt him to issue, in the sixth year of his reign, a royal order

1. *Tarikh-i-Salim Shahi* (Calcutta Edition), pp.21-22.
2. *Ibid.,* pp. 41-41.
3. For this conclusion see K.S.Lal, *Growth of Muslim Population in Medeival India,* p.143.

prohibiting the provincial governors from converting any one forcibly to Islam.[1] Jahangir also discouraged making of eunuchs in Bengal for being presented to the court[2] (for service in the Mughal harem and ultimately becoming Muhammadans). But he was not against peaceful encouragement to conversions.[3] Some prisoners were also offered pardon if they turned Musalman.[4]

In one respect alone Jahangir deviated from the policy of his father: he did not permit people to embrace Hinduism even of their own free will. He severely punished Kaukab, Sharif and Abdul Latif who, under the influence of a Sanyasi, showed inclination for Hinduism.[5] This policy would have stopped any erosion of Muslim numbers. Besides, while on a visit to Kashmir, when he learnt that the Hindus and Muslims intermarried freely, "and both give and take girls (he ordered that) taking them is good but giving them, God Forbid".[6] And any violation of this order was to be visited with capital punishment.[7] This indeed was in accordance with the Islamic law. As per the Shariat law a Muslim may marry a Jewess, or a Christian, or a Sabean, but "a marriage between a Musalman and ... a Hindu is invalid". Similarly, " a female Muslim cannot under any circumstances marry a non-Muslim".[8] So, Jahangir was being unnecessarily fussy, because, whether a Muslim married a Hindu girl or

1. *Tuzuk-i-Jahangiri*, or *Memoirs of Jahangir*, I, p.205.
2. *Ibid.*, I, pp.150-151.
3. Aziz Ahmad, *Studies in Islamic Culture...*,p.83.
4. Sri Ram Sharma, *The Religious Policy of the Mughal Emperors*, pp.61-62.
5. *Tuzuk-i-Jahangiri*, I, p.171.
6. *Ibid.*, II, p.181.
7. *Loc. cit.*

May be it was because of this that Akbar discouraged all kinds of intercommunal marriages. Badaoni, *Muntakhab-ut-Tawarikh*, II, p.413. Also *Ain-i-Akbari*, Blochmann, I, p.220.

8. Hughes, *Dictionary of Islam*, p.318 and Ram Swarup, *Understanding Islam through Hadis*, p.59.

a Hindu married a Muslim girl, in course of time all of them used to become Muhammadan. Shahjahan's orders in this regard were that the Hindus could keep their Muslim wives only if they accepted Islam. Consequently, during his reign, 4,000 to 5,000 Hindus converted to Islam in Bhadnor alone.[1] Seventy such cases were found in Gujarat and 400 in the Punjab.[2] The policy of converting such "families" would have contributed to the growth of Muslim numbers.

Shahjahan was even otherwise interested in making converts. Professor Sri Ram Sharma has collected facts and figures of Hindus converted to Islam from the works of Qazvini, Lahori, Salih, Mohsin Fani, Khafi Khan, etc. during Shajahan's reign and has thus saved me the labour of doing the same. The following is the summary of what he says. "Early in his reign Shahjahan had appointed a Superintendent of converts to Islam, thus setting up a department for the special purpose of making converts. The one common practice was to make terms with the criminals... The Hindus of the Punjab, Bhimbar, Bhadauri and Sirhind...were all offered remission of their sentences provided they accepted the 'true faith'. When the war with the Portuguese started, of the 400 prisoners taken a few became Muslims. The rest were kept in prison with orders that whenever they expressed willingness to embrace Islam, they were to be converted, liberated and given daily allowances.[3] An order was issued in the seventh year of his reign that if a Hindu wanted to be converted to Islam, his family should not place any obstacles in his way... Under Shahjahan, apostasy from Islam had again become a capital crime."[4]

1. Qazvini, *Badshah Nama*, pp.444-45; Lahori, *Badshah Nama* , 2 vols. (Calcutta 1876); Khafi Khan, *Muntakhab-ul-Lubab*. I, p.510.
2. Sharma, *op. cit.*, pp.88-89 and Sharma, *Conversion and Re-conversion to Hinduism* (D.A.V. College Historical series No.2 n.d.) also Qazvini, p.562.
3. Also Lahori, *op. cit.*, I, p.534.
4. Sharma, *op. cit.*, pp.90-91.

Some other practices discontinued by Akbar were revived by Shahjahan. Forcible conversion during war became common in his reign. "When Shuja was appointed governor of Kabul (he carried on) a ruthless war in the Hindu territory beyond the Indus... Sixteen sons and dependants of Hathi were converted by force. The sword of Islam further yielded a crop of Muslim converts... The rebellion of Jujhar Singh yielded a rich crop of Muslim converts, mostly minors. His young son Durga and his grandson Durjan Sal were both converted to become Imam Quli and Ali Quli[1]... Most of the women had burnt themselves...but such as were captured – probably slave girls and maids – were converted and distributed among Muslim Mansabdars[2]... The conquest of Beglana was followed by conversion of Naharji's son...who now became Daulatmand."[3]

Akbar had prohibited enslavement and sale of women and children of peasants who had defaulted in payment of revenue. He knew, as Abul Fazl says, that many evil hearted and vicious men either because of ill-founded suspicion or sheer greed, used to proceed to villages and mahals and sack them.[4] But under Shahjahan conditions worsened. Now peasants were compelled to sell their women and children to meet the revenue demand.[5] Manrique writes that the peasants "are carried off... to various markets and fairs (to be sold), with their poor unhappy wives behind them carrying their small children... all crying and lamenting..."[6] Accoring to Qazvini, Shahjahan's orders in this regard were that

1. Lahori, I, ii, p.133.
2. *Ibid.*, p.139. Khafi Khan, *op. cit.*, I, pp.522-23.
3. Sharma, *op. cit.*, p.91.
4. *Akbar Nama*, trs. H. Beveridge, 3 vols (Calcutta, 1948), II, p.451.
5. Manucci, *Storia do Mogor*, 4 vols., II, p.451.
6. Manrique, *Travels of Frey Sebastian Manrique*, 2 vols., II, p.272. Also see Bernier, *Travels in the Mogul Empire*.

captives were not to be sold to Hindus as slaves,[1] and under Muslim customers they could only become Musalman.

Under Shahjahan, therefore, active steps were taken to swell the number of Muslims. He is praised by all contemporary Persian chroniclers as a great Muslim king who was anxious to restore the prestige of Islam. But proselytization to Islam as such could not be extensive under Shahjahan. He was not a royal missionary like Sultan Firoz Tughlaq, Sikandar Butshikan, Jalaluddin of Bengal, Mahmud Beghara of Gujarat or the Emperor Aurangzeb. In spite of certain deviations, the catholic spirit of Akbar's government had not been lost under Jahangir and Shahjahan.[2] Dara Shukoh was Shahjahan's favourite son, and his nearness to the throne would have imparted an unorthodox colour to administration.

Indeed, it appears that from about the middle of the sixteenth to the middle of the seventeenth century, conversions to Islam were not done on a very large scale. Bernier, who was in India towards the closing years of Shahjahan's and early years of Aurangzeb's reign found India a country of vast majority of Hindus. He even goes on to say: "The great Mogol is a foreigner in Hindoustan, he finds himself in a hostile country, or nearly so; a country containing hundreds of Gentiles to one Mogol, or even to one Mahometan."[3] Being a foreigner, Bernier might not have been able to quite distinguish between Hindus and Muslims. In any case, as Beni Prased points out, "he (Bernier) wrote from mere observation and made no systematic calculation."[4] Nevertheless, Bernier's impression is similar to the observations of men like

1. Qazvini, *op. cit.*, p.405.
2. Bernier, *op. cit.*, p.306.
3. *Ibid.*, p.209.
4. Beni Prasad, 'India in 1605 A.C.' *Modern Review* (Calcutta, January 1921), pp.15-22, p.17n.

Timur and Babur and many other foreign writers.[1] What is of importance about Bernier's assertion is that in spite of some conversions in the countryside, the demographic complexion of the society in which he lived and moved had not perhaps registered any appreciable change in the Hindu-Muslim proportion since the days of Babur.

But with the coming into power of Aurangzeb a spate of conversions followed. "The proselytizing activity of Aurangzeb seems to have started about the year 1666 (the year of Shahjahan's death in prison), and remained unabated till the end of his life."[2] He tried his utmost to raise the number of Muslims by all possible means.

In April 1667, four revenue collectors (*qanungos*), who had been dismissed for various faults, were reinstated on their accepting the Muhammadan faith.[3] Aurangzeb's declared policy of "*Qanungo basharte Islam*"[4] (Qanungoship on the conditon of conversion to Islam) brought many converts and many Muslim families in Punjab still retain the letter of reinstatement on conversion or fresh appointment of Muslims in place of Hindu Qanungos who were retrenched because they would not

1. Early in the seventeenth century, Muhammad Sharif Hanafi, the author of *Majalis-us-Salatin* (composed C.E.1628) and a much travelled man, carried the same impression about the Southern region of the country. Writing about Carnatic he says: "All the people... are idolaters. There is not a single Musalman. Occasionally a Musalman may visit the country deputed by Nizam Shah, Adil Shah or Kutb Shah, but the natives are all infidels." E. and D., VII, p.139.
2. S.R. Sharma, *op. cit.*, p.165. Professor Sharma has again come to my rescue by collecting facts and figures of conversions from the original sources of Aurangzeb's reign including News Letters (*Akhbarat*) and royal correspondence. Sharma pp.165-174. Since it is a matter of facts and figures and not of "interpretation", or opinion, there need be no hesitation in accepting them.
3. Sharma, *op. cit.*, p.165.
4. K.R. Qanungo, *Historical Essays*, p.ii.

convert.[1] Such cases belong to places from the Punjab to Bengal which shows that the policy was followed throughout the length and breadth of the county.[2] Government appointments and promotions on conversion, too, were of frequent occurrences. Nam Dev was, on conversion, appointed to the command of 400; and Shiva Singh, a grandson of Raja Kishan Das of Amroha was, on becoming Musalman, appointed Musharaf of Imtiazgarh. The *News Letters* mention conversion of Nek Ram, who rose to acquire the title of a Raja, and Dilawar, who is spoken of as a commander of 1000.

Tempting offers were given to high and low to embrace Islam. Even Rajas and Zamindars could not resist such temptation. A brother of the Zamindar of Dev Garh converted to Muhammadanism and became Islam Yar. He was given the Zamindari, superseding the existing chief. Some others like Zorawar Singh and Shyam Singh of the same estate followed suit.[3] Devi Chand, a Zamindar of Manoharpur, who had been dismissed from his mansab, was restored to it on becoming Musalman. There are many other similar cases.[4] Shankarji, the Zamindar of Pataudi, and Fateh Singh son of Raja Ram the Jat leader, and the son of Gokal Jat were converted, the last one after his father's death. Bishan Narayan, son of Raja Shiv Narayan of Kuch Bihar, was admitted to Islam while Aurangzeb's armies were busy in an expedition against his father. Kondaji, uncle of Netoji was also converted in the tenth year of the reign. The Raja of Palamau was offered better terms if he would accept Islam. Manucci mentions the case of three Rajas, who got appointments at the imperial court on conversion.[5] These are

1. J.N. Sarkar, *Aurangzeb.*
2. Sharma, *op. cit.*, pp.169-173.
3. *Ibid.*, p.166.
4. *Loc. cit.*
5. Manucci, II, p. 436.

individual instances, but many loyal servants and subjects of the Rajas and Zamindars would have followed suit and embraced Islam when their masters became Musalman.

The poor converted more easily and in larger numbers. Of the temptations given for conversion were an audience with the Emperor, a robe of Honour, and a daily allowance which generally ranged from four annas to seven rupees[1]; even four annas was a high amount in those days. A Deccanese was converted to Islam and given Rs. 2,000.[2] Obviously economic inducement was a great temptation for the poor. Criminals were given remission from sentence if they converted to Islam. The *Maasir-i-Alamgiri* mentions a case in which a Hindu clerk killed the seducer of his sister, but escaped execution by embracing Islam.[3] There were many more similar cases.[4] In September, 1681, an order was issued that all prisoners who would accept Islam were to be set at liberty.[5] The practice was so common that no other specific cases need be mentioned.

Imposition of the Jiziyah brought a better crop of converts. We have seen that under Firoz Tughlaq the strict imposition of Jiziyah had compelled many people to become Musalmans. Akbar had abolished it, but under Aurangzeb this "econmic pressure" was revived. Manucci notes that the Jiziyah was instituted "to force the Hindus to become Muhammedans, to obtain relief from the insults of the collectors..."[6] Aurangzeb "was of the opinion that he

1. Sharma, p.170.
2. *Alamgir Nama,* p.567 cited in Sharma p.173.
3. Mustaad Khan, *Maasir-i-Alamgiri,* Eng. trs. Jadunath Sarkar (Calcutta, 1947), p.73.
4. Sharma, *op. cit.*, pp.170-172. Rizqullah mentions the case of a thief who converted to Islam and was given charge of a city. *Waqiat-i-Mushtaqi*, fols. 13b-14a.
5. News Letter of even date, cited in Sharma, p.166.
6. Manucci, *op. cit.*, II, 234.

had found in this tax an excellent means of succeeding in converting them".[1] Customs duties on the Hindu traders were increased; on Muslims abolished.[2] If the economic stress could make some people convert just for a stipend of four annas a day, how many more would have accepted Islam on account of the compulsions of the Jiziyah.

The enslavement of women and children too was a common phenomenon now. The practice was revived under Shahjahan; it had not probably been abolished completely earlier. An interesting piece of information supplied by Manucci should suffice here. He gives a long list of women dancers, singers and slave-girls like Hira Bai, Sundar Bai, Nain-jot Bai, Chanchal Bai, Apsara Bai, Khushhal Bai, Kesar Bai, Gulal, Champa, Chameli, Saloni, Madhumati, Koil, Menhdi, Moti, Kishmish, Pista etc., etc., and adds: "All the above names are Hindu, and ordinarily these... are Hindus by race, who had been carried off in infancy from various villages or the houses of different rebel Hindu princes. In spite of their Hindu names, they are, however, Mohamedans".[3] It appears that the number of such converts was so large that even their Hindu names could not be changed to Islamic.[4] The policy of enslavement and conversion was also followed by others of smaller note. Sidi Yaqut of Janjira once took a Maratha fort after granting quarter to the garrison. Seven hundred persons came out. Notwithstanding his word, "he made the children and pretty women slaves, and forcibly converted them to Islam...but the men he put to death."[5]

---

1. *Ibid.*, III, pp.288-89, also IV, p.117. Also most Persian chroniclers.
2. *Ibid.*, II, p.415.
3. *Ibid.*, II, pp.336, 337-338. Also Lal, *The Mughal Harem*, pp.29-32; 165-67. For instances of enslavement by Aurangzeb see Khafi Khan E and D. VII, pp.300, 371.
4. See K.S. Lal, *The Mughal Harem* (New Delhi, 1988), pp.167-169.
5. Khafi Khan, *op. cit.*, II, p.228.

Thus Aurangzeb's proselytizing zeal resulted in good number of conversions. He seems to have employed all the means at his disposal to raise Muslim population. In the dispute about estates between two brothers or relatives, the Raja or Zamindar who embraced Islam was given the property. Other kinds of pressures or temptations brought other Rajas into the fold of Islam.[1] Criminals were set free if they became Muslims. Economic pressure of Jiziyah and inducement of jobs brought in may more converts. Enslavement too was a contributory factor. Then there was sheer force – force by the king, his nobles and local officers. There are references in the reports forwarded by Kotwals and Faujdars about their efforts and achievements in making converts in their jurisdiction. The forcible conversion of Frontier Tribes by Aurangzeb is a well-known fact. "Popular Hindu and Sikh tradition ascribes mass conversions by force to Aurangzeb's reign."[2] Christians too were forcibly converted to Islam.[3] Both offcial and non-official sources point to a high rate of conversion, much above the normal. Naturally Aurangzeb seems to have been satisfied with his achievements. Manucci says that just before the emperor died , he said: "I die happy for at least the world will be able to say that I have employed every effort to destroy the enemies of the Muhammedan faith."[4]

Although the actual addition to Muslim numbers because of Aurangzeb's all-embracing campaign for proselytization is difficult to compute, yet his pronouncements, his enthusiasm, his collection of day-to-day information about conversions, his personally instructing the neo-converts in the tenets of Islamic faith, and his ultimate satisfaction at his success together with the information

1. Manucci, *op. cit.*, II, p.436.
2. Sharma, p.168.
3. Manucci, *op. cit.*, II, p.404.
4. *Ibid.*, IV, p.398.

contained in contemporary writings, do show clearly that addition to Muslim population during his reign was substantial.

After Aurangzeb's death the spate of conversions abated. The Royal Princes got busy in wars of succession, the chief nobles in capturing power or carving out independent kingdoms. From the description of wars during the early part of the eighteenth century, aimed at succession or independence, it appears that they resulted in Muslim losses mainly, because "the descendants of Aurangzeb could not persuade one (Rajput) to strike a blow in defence of his throne."[1] Repeated appeals made by the contending parties that Muslim lives should not be wasted in futile warfare, is not without significance.[2] It is at least obvious that in such wars Hindu captives or converts could not be obtained.

Invasions of Nadir Shah and Ahmad Shah Abdali added to the loss in Muslim numbers. Disgruntled Muslim nobles and religious leaders used to implore foreign invaders to attack India. Babur was invited and so were Nadir Shah and Ahmad Shah Abdali. Such Indian Muslims had little consideration for the overall interests of the countrymen as a whole. These invaders killed more Hindus than Muslims; but of course Muslims were also killed in large numbers. The effects of Nadir's march through the Punjab, his massacre at Delhi which cost thousands of Muslim lives,[3] and Abdali's sack of the Punjab not less than eight times between 1748 and 1769,[4] on Indian and especially Muslim demography need

1. C.H.I., IV, p.358.
2. E.g. Khafi Khan, *op. cit.*, pp.396, 452, 496, 542.
3. C.H.I., IV, p.361 and n.2.
4. Shaikh Abdur Rashid, *Najibuddaullah, His Life and Times*, (Cosmopolitan Publishers, Aligarh, 1952), Introduction, pp.xlix-li. Also see Irvine, *Indian Antiquary*, Vol.36, 1907, pp.46ff.

not be stressed. Even Delhi, the imperial capital, could not recover from the shocks right up to the end of thecentury.[1]

However, during this period a good number of Afghans had migrated to India, compensating to some extent the loss of Muslim population. In the region comprising the modern districts of Bijnor, Moradabad, Badaon, Bareilly, Shahjahanpur, Rohilla Afghans had started settling in the seventeenth century.[2] "Sometime during the reign of Shahjahan, Daud Zai Afghans (had) settled in this tract and founded the important town of Shahjahanpur." But in the eighteenth century, while the rise of Nadir Shah scattered the Afghans in their own country and many of them came to India, the disturbed political state of India and the anxiety of the different leaders to secure military assistance of the warlike Afghans provided the necessary openings which the Afghans well utilized.[3] Thus the displacement from Qandhar and the country around by Nadir Shah and the pull exercised by the political vacuum caused by the rapid decline of the Mughal empire resulted in the immigration of a goodly number of Afghans.[4] By the middle of the eighteenth century Najibuddaulah, a Yusufzai Rohilla Nawab in India, declared on the eve of the battle of Panipat (1761) that he could depend upon the support of 150,000 Afghans who were in India.[5]

But for the compensating immigration, the resources of the Mughal empire in the eighteenth century rapidly declined and economic temptations could not be offered to obtain converts. Jiziyah was officially abolished in 1719-20.[6] It was only a formal recognition of the fact that it

1. W. Francklin. *The History of the Reign of Shah-Aulum,* pp.200-201.
2. Jadunath Sarkar, *Fall of the Mughal Empire, op. cit.*, I, pp.27-28.
3. Abdur Rashid, *Najibuddaulah, op. cit.*, Intro. xxxii, liii.
4. *Ibid.*, liii-iv.
5. *Ibid.*, lxxvi.
6. Khafi Khan, p.479.

could not be collected after Aurangzeb's death.[1] In independent Muslim states, which had been fighting against Aurangzeb or had emerged with the decline of the Mughal empire, the effort was to seek the goodwill of the Hindus rather than to annoy them with any compaign for proselytization.[2]

Moreover, the Hindus – Jats, Marathas, Sikhs, and Rajputs – had gathered strength. By 1719 when the Faujdari of Surat was held by Raja Jai Singh and the Subedaris of Ahmedabad and Ajmer, including Jodhpur, by Ajit Singh, "the two Rajas held all the country from thirty kos of Delhi...to the shores of the sea at Surat."[3] The power of the Rajputs can be guaged from certain acts of Ajit Singh.[4] In the Punjab, Banda Bahadur's activities were continued by his successors until the Sikhs became masters of the Punjab, and they in place of permitting any further erosion of Hindu numbers, converted people to their own creed, 'sometimes by force.'[5] The power of the Marathas already established in the South, began to be extended to the North, so that by the middle of the eighteenth century, Rustam Ali, who was compelled to "travel from city to city in search of employment and subsistence", writes in his *Tarikh-i-Hind* (composed C.E. 1741-42) that "from the day he left Shah Jahanabad (Delhi),

1. *Ibid.*, pp.462, 516, 524, also *Kanz-ul-Mahfuz*, E and D, VIII, p.39.
2. Khafi Khan, *op. cit.*, p.325.
3. *Ibid.*, p.485.
4. "Maharaja Ajit Singh took back the Maharani, his daughter, who had been married to Farrukh Siyar, with all her Jewels...he made her throw off her Musalman dress, dismissed her Muhammadan attendants and sent her to her native country...In the reign of no former Emperor had any Raja been so presumptous as to take his daughter after she had been married to a king and admitted to the honour of Islam." Khafi Khan, *op. cit.*, p.483. Probably this is not an isolated case of reconversion to Hinduism.
5. Khafi Khan, *op. cit.*, p.419.

and travelled through the country of idolatry, it was here (at Bhopal) only that he found Islam to be predominant."[1]

In these circumstances, the spate of conversions to Islam slackened. Some stray efforts at conversion no doubt continued to be made even during the eighteenth century, but without much success. For instance when in 1716 Banda Bahadur with his 740 followers was given by Farrukh Siyar the choice between Islam and death, they all died to a man rather than become Musalman.[2] Similarly, according to T.W. Arnold, Tipu Sultan issued an order to the people of Malabar to becαme Musalmans, "and early in 1789 (he) prepared to enforce his proclamation with an army of more than twenty thousand men...Thousands of Hindus were accordingly circumcised and made to eat beef; but this monarch himself perished, early in 1799...Most of the Brahmans and Nayars who had been forcibly converted subsequently disowned their new religion."[3] However, Tipu Sultan declared that his conversion compaign had been very successful and that on a single occasion, within twentyfour hours he caused swelling in the ranks of the faithful by 50,000. All along his invasion route in Kerala, over 500 Hindu temples were desecrated by his armies in Cannanore, Calicut and Mallapuram districts. Some of the ruins are still extent. However, from all the evidence available, it appears that

---

1. E and D, VIII, p.58.
2. C.H.I., IV, *op. cit.*, p.335.

Some people would have been converted during the invasions of Nadir Shah and Ahmad Shah Abdali. Muhammad Aslam in his *Farhat-un-Nazirin* says that during the Third Battle of Panipat (1761) about 90, 000 persons, "male and female, were taken prisoner and obtained eternal happiness by embracing the Muhammadan faith", *op. cit.*, p.171... But not only is he not supported by any other contemporary historians, the very incidents of the war militate against such large-scale conversions.

3. Arnold, *The Preaching of Islam*, pp.261 ff cited in Titus, *Islam in India and Pakistan*, p.33.

Muslim population did not register rise in the eighteenth century through proselytization. On the contrary, there was perhaps a recession even in its natural growth due to disturbed political conditions in which Muslim numbers seem to have suffered a shrinkage.

To conclude: while the total population of India from 1000 to 1800 had registered rise and fall by turns, Muslim population had shown only a constant rise. In 1000 Muslim numbers in India were microscopic. In 1200 they were perhaps about three to four hundred thousand. By 1400 their number had risen probably to 3.2 million and they formed about 1.85 percent of the total population. In 1600 they were probably 15 million. And from the 1: 9 to 1: 10 Muslim-Hindu ratio in 1600 the proportion of Muslims to Hindus had gone up to about 1: 7 by the year 1800. When Bishop Heber wrote his journal (1826), his inquiries pointed to a Muslim-Hindu ratio of 1:6.[1] Edward Thornton's Gazetteer[2] published in 1854 also gives the ratio of 1: 6. Thus at about the middle of the ninteenth century, the Muslim-Hindu ratio stood approximately at 1: 6. This would make the Muslims 16 per cent of the total population. In 1800 this percentage was obviously less – 15 or even 14. The total population estimated for C.E. 1800 is 170 millions.[2] Muslims who were 15 percent of the total would have been about 25 millions. By the end of the nineteenth century, the ratio had changed to 1: 5, and Stanely Lanepoole, whose *Medieval India* was first published in 1903, rightly observes: "The population of India in the present day is over three hundred millions, and every sixth man is a Muslim."[3] The total population of India, according to 1901 Census was 283,867,584 (including persons in the N.W. Frontier Province) and

1. Heber's *Narrative of a Journey*. Also see J.M. Datta, *Modern Review*, January, 1918, pp.33-34.
2. Lal, *Growth of Muslim Population... op. cit.*, p.15.
3. S. Lanepoole, *Medieval India*, p.1.

Muslims numbered 62,861,542.[1] Therefore, approximately every sixth person was a Muslim and the ratio stood at 1: 5. And since Muslim numbers in proportion to the Hindus have increased progressively through decades and centuries, a ratio of 1: 6 for the middle of the nineteenth and 1: 7 for the year 1800 is not only a fair estimate but almost a correct figure for which evidence is available in Thornton's Gazetteer and its authentic sources.[2]

1. See Census Report for 1901 and Kingsley Davis, *The Population of India and Pakistan*, p.179, Table 77.

2. Robert Orme's estimates are low both for the Muslim population as well as for the total population of India. His assessment of the Hindu-Muslim proportion also does not seem to be correct. What he writes is this: "From these origins time has formed in India a nation of near ten million of Mohamdans whom the Europeans call Moor, to them under the authority of the Great Mogul, the greatest part of Hindustan is now subject; but although the reigning nation, they are outnumbered by the Indians ten to one." Robert Orme, *A History of the Millitary Transactions of the British Nation in Indostan*, 3 vols. 4th ed. (London, 1803), I, p.24.

Chapter 5

Factors Contributing to the Growth of Muslim Population

A study of the preceding pages clearly shows that the rise in Muslim population was due mainly to conversions of Hindus to Islam. It also needs no reiteration that "it was part of the state policy to establish Islam as the religion of the whole land".[1] It would again be a truism to say that "Islam is essentially a missionary religion" and every Muslim is a propagandist of his faith; and as they settled in India, they must have entered upon proselytizing efforts.[2] Thus Muslim rulers, nobels, Mashaikh, Maulvis, traders and merchants were all in one way or the other Muslim missionaries.

Conversions

Islam has spread in many parts of the world through wars and campaigns. In the medieval Indian chronicles the sovereign is always mentioned as 'the king of Islam', the territories of his empire are referred to as the 'land of Islam', its armies as 'soldiers of Islam', and its religious and Judicial head as 'Shaikh-ul-Islam'. The monarch was committed to make Islam the true basis of private and public life through the enforcement of the Shariat and to convert the people to the "true faith". In India the Muslim rulers' keenness to obtain converts in war is vouched by many chroniclers. The *Tarikh-i-Muhammadi* gives a clear idea of the psychology of the rulers in this regard. Its

1. Titus, *op. cit.*, p.32.
2. Tara chand, *op. cit.*, p.33.

author was a contemporary of Sultan Nasiruddin Mahmud, the son of Firoz Tughlaq. He says that while fighting Rai Subir (Sumer) in the vicinity of Iraj, the Sultan thought: "If I will give orders to the army to fight (outright), they will not leave even a trace of the Kafirs in the region, but if I shall advance slowly, then probably these people will agree to embrace Islam."[1] What professor Mohammad Habib writes concerning the Mongol applies equally to Turkish expeditions. "In 1330 the country was invaded by the Mongols who indulged in arson, rape and murder througout the Valley (of Kashmir). The king and the Brahmans fled away but among the inhabitants who remained...Muslim ways of life were gradually adopted by the people as the only alternative..."[2] Thus warfare brought captives, and captives were made Musalmans. Such was not the situation only in the North; in South also such methods of conversion prevailed, especially during wars between Bahmani and Vijayanagar kingdoms. Throughtout the medieval period such wars were common, and forcible conversions helped in the rapid growth of Muslim population.

The rulers used force and persuasion in equal measure. Their resources were great. They could give jobs, honours, and titles and many other economic concessions and status benefits as inducements to conversion, and many people would have taken advantage of these facilities. We have referred to Mubarak Khalji's encouragement to Hindus to accept Islam by presenting the convert with a robe and a gold ornament. People used to be converted in this fashion right up to the reign of Aurangzeb and perhaps even thereafter. There were other methods too.

1. Muhammad Bihamid Khani, *Tarikh-i-Muhammadi*, British Museum Ms. 440 b, trans. into Hindi by A.A. Rizvi in *Uttar Timur Kalin Bharat*, Pt. II (Aligarh, 1959), p.30.
2. Mohammad Habib, *Some Aspects of the Foundation of the Delhi Sultanate*, *op. cit.*, p.20

The *Banshasmriti* of Satya Krishna Biswas states that in Bengal the Rajas and Zamindars who could not deposit land revenue by a certain date had to convert to Muhammadanism. The *Banshasmriti* narrates an isolated incident, but as this regulation of the thirteenth century had been revived by Murshid Quli Khan, or had continued right up to his times, many local Rajas and Zamindars would have been converted in the course of four centuries, for full payment of land tax by due date was not always possible. Firoz Tughlaq (1351-88) instructed his revenue collectors to convert Hindus to Islām.[1] He rescinded the Jiziyah to lure people to become Muhammadans, and this measure brought large additions to Muslim population. In his *Fatuhat-i-Firoz Shahi,* Sultan Firoz Tughlaq candidly writres: "I encouraged my infidel subjects to embrace the religion of the prophet and I proclaimed that everyone who repeated the *Kalima of tauhid* and became Musalman should be exempt from Jiziyah... Information of this came to the ears of the people at large, and great number of Hindus presented themselves, and were admitted to the honour of Islam. Thus they came forward day by day from every quarter, go on coming to this day, and adopting the faith, are exonerated from the Jiziyah, and are favoured with Khilats and presents."[2]

Side by side the goverment's efforts was the proselytizing activity of the Muslim Sufis. It is however not clear how far Sūfi and other Mashaikh were interested in the work of conversion and what amount of success they achieved in this regard. Following in the footsteps of T.W. Arnold,[3] Titus, Aziz Ahmad and Mujeeb assert that conversions to Islam were mainly a result of the labours of the

1. Afif, *op. cit.,* pp.268-269.
Also Ishwari Prasad, *Qaraunah Turks, op.cit.,* p.331.
2. *Fatuhat-i-Firoz Shahi,* trs. in E and D, III, p.368. Also Hindi trs. Rizvi, *Tughlaq Kalin Bharat,* II, (Aligarh, 1957), p.337.
3. T.W. Arnold, *The Preaching of Islam, op. cit.,* pp.264ff.

mystics.[1] Perhaps the idea is to prove that the conversions were voluntary. On the other hand Mohammad Habib and S.A.A. Rizvi say that Sufi Mashaikh were not engaged in effecting conversions. Prof. Habib says, "The Musalmans have no missionary labours to record... *We find no trace of any missionary movement for converting non-Muslims* (italics by the author himself). Medieval Islam was a converting creed, but it failed to develop any missionary activity... So far as our country is concerned we have to confess frankly that no trace of a missionary movement for the conversion of non-Muslims has yet been discovered." In a footnote he adds: "Some cheap mystic books now current attribute conversions to Muslim mystics on the basis of miracles they performed. So in order to believe in the conversions one has to believe in the miracles also. But all such books will be found on examination to be latter-day fabrications."[2] Prof. Rizvi arrives at the same conclusion. He simply says that "the early mystic records (*Malfuzat* and *Maktubat*), contain no mention of conversion of the people to Islam by these Saints."[3]

From the hagiological literature also it is evident that Sufi Mashaikh were not organized for propaganda work in any modern way.[4] Sufi Shaikhs and scholars are not known to have preceded but always followed the armies of invasion.[5] They mostly lived in metropolitan cities, in their respective *Khanqahs* or monasteries, basking in the sunshine of royal favour, and do not appear to have moved about in the countryside for propaganda work.

1. Titus, *op. cit.*, Chapter III entitled "Peaceful Penetration", pp.36-53. Aziz Ahmad, *Studies in Islamic Culture*, pp.81-84. Mujeeb, *op. cit.*, p.22.
2. K.M. Ashraf Memorial Lecture, *op. cit.*, pp.18-19. Also P.M. Currie, *Cult of Muin-al-din Chishti of Ajmer* (Oxford, Delhi, 1989)
3. S.A.A. Rizvi, *Muslim Revivalist Movements in Northern India in the Sixteenth and Seventeenth Centuries* (Agra University, 1965), p.18.
4. Titus, *op. cit.*, p.42.
5. *Ibid.*, p.44.

The whole atmosphere in the *Khanqah* was Muslim: not many, if any, Hindus ever visited them, not to speak of their coming in large numbers for being converted.[1] The two greatest Chishti Mashaikh of the medieval period were Muin-ud-din Chishti and Nizam-ud-din Auliya Rizvi rightly says that Shaikh Muin-ud-din Chishti "was neither a missionary nor a miracle monger. He did not work among the masses..."[2] In the *Fawaid-ul-Fuad,* a biographical memoir on Shaikh Nizam-ud-din Auliya, there is mention of conversion of only two Hindu curd-sellers. Similarly during the reign of Iltutmish, Khwaja Qutubuddin Bakhtiyar Kaki and Qazi Hamid-ud-din Nagori were two prominent saints in Delhi but no proselytizing activity is attributed to them.[3] Indeed the Mashaikh sometimes resented government's appeals to do proselytizing work; and Muhammad bin Tughlaq, who wanted to employ this class on missionary work, met with lot of opposition from them.[4]

In brief, while it would not be safe to declare that hardly any conversions through peaceful methods were effected by the Sufi Mashaikh in India, it has also to be admitted that not many reliable references to their proselytizing activity are available in genuine hagiological works. They may have helped those who showed an inclination to become Muslim. Occasionally they restored to force also to convert people.[5] But the Mashaikh were

1. Rizvi, *op. cit.,* p.20., P.M. Currie, *The Shrine and Cult of Muin-al-din-Chishti of Ajmer* (OUP, 1989), pp.20-96, esp. pp.29-30.
2. Rizvi, *op. cit.,* p.15.
3. Ferishtah, I, pp.66-67.
4. Mahdi Husain, *Tughlaq Dynasty,* pp.149-50, 160 and also p.174 and n.2-3 Also see Kirmani, *Siyar-ul-Auliya,* p.228.
5. As for instance the efforts of Raju Qattal to convert Nahawan, the Darogha of Ucch. Jamali, *Siyar-ul-Arifin* (Delhi, 1311H), pp.159-60. Also Ferishtah, *op. cit.,* II, pp.417-18. Eaton, *Sufis of Bijapur,* esp. Chapter entitled 'Sufi Warriors'. Also see their militant proselytizing activity in Bengal in Chapter 3.

probably responsible only for stray and individual conversions and their contribution to the growth of Muslim population may not have been much. Saiyyad Muhammad bin Nasiruddin Jafar Makki al-Husaini , the Khalifa of Nasiruddin Chiragh-i-Delhi "held that there were five reasons which led the people to embrace Islam:

(1) Fear of death,

(2) fear of their families being enslaved,

(3) propagation (of Islam) on the part of Muslims,

(4) the lust for obtaining *mawajib* (pensions or rewards) *ghanaim* (booty), and

(5) Tassub (bigotry or superstition?)."[1]

Thus, according to Saiyyad Muhammad, propagation of Islam by Muslims did not necessarily involve missionary activity of Sufi Mashaikh. Prior to its introduction in India, Islam had spread in many other countries like Arabia, Persia and Syria. No names of missionaries or Sufi saints have come down to us as having been instrumental in spreading Islam in those countries. It is only about India that such a therory is put forward.

Today many classes or groups of people who were originally Hindu are found to belong to the Muhammadan faith, and their conversion can be traced to medieval times. An oft-repeated reason for such conversions is said to be the tyranny of the Hindu caste system. Arnold, Titus and Aziz Ahmad give credit to "the democratic social system of Islam"[2] for the conversion of low caste Hindus to "win a degree of social freedom" because "for the lower Hindu castes acceptance of Islam meant an escape from the degraded status they had in the Hindu society."[3] Dr. Wise thinks that the Muhammadan Julaha (Jolha or Momin) weaver class of Bengal and Bihar belonged to a

1. Rizvi, *op. cit.*, p.46 citing Sijzi, *Akhbar-ul-Akhiyar*, p.136.
2. Titus, *op. cit.*, p.36.
3. Aziz Ahmad, *op. cit.*, p.82.

"despised Hindu caste who in a body became converts to Muhammedanism." Ruben Levy also talks of the "coarse rabble" or Ajlaf in Bengal, who formed the functional groups such as weavers, cotton carders, oil pressers, barbers, tailors etc., as well as converts of originally humble castes in Bengal.[1]

However, contemporary writings of Persian chroniclers nowhere mention caste as a factor leading to conversions. Muslim historians of medieval India were surely aware of the existence of the caste system in Hindu society; Alberuni, Abul Fazl and emperor Jahangir, to mention a few. And yet no one mentions even once tyranny on the low caste people as cause for conversion. Their evidence shows beyond doubt that conversions in India were brought about by the same methods and processes as seen in Arabia, Persia, Central Asia, etc. India was not the first country where Islam was introduced in medieval times. It had spread in Persia, Central Asia, Afghanistan, and North Africa before it came to India. There was no caste system in these countries and yet there were large-scale conversions there.

Therefore, a little reflection off the beaten track would show that the reason behind the conversion of some groups *en masse* was not due to the assumed oppression of the caste system but to escape oppressive taxes and other disabilities. Conversion also provided new avenues of employment and economic advancement in the Muslim regime and society. Naturally large numbers of poor people were attracted to Islam as the following Table, prepared on the basis of U.P. Census Report of 1931, indicates.

1. Ruben Levy, *The Social Structure of Islam* (Cambridge, 1957), p.73.

Table
Showing Some Muslim Low Castes of U.P.[1]

	Per cent of caste members adhering to Muslim Religion	Per cent of each Caste in Total Religious Membership
Julaha	95.5	14.7
Faqir	93.0	12.9
Dhunia	93.5	5.4
Teli	25.1	3.4
Nai (Hajjam)	26.9	3.3
Darzi	69.5	2.3
Qassab	100.0	2.2
Dhobi	14.0	1.5
Manihar	96.4	1.4

Like U.P. functional groups many occupational groups in other parts of the country, especially in northern India, too went over to Islam in large numbers in medieval times. Now, did the ancestors of the above Muslim castes convert in medieval times because of the tyranny of the caste system? Let us take the Faqirs first. In Hindu society there is no 'caste' of beggars. But any number of beggars would be 'born' if they could get free food without doing any work. It is stated in almost every chronicle that in medieval times food was very cheap, even then, many idlers would have avoided to do work if they could get free food just for a change of name – religion of the poor being the proverbial bread. Muslim regime provided it

1. Compiled from the Census Report of India, 1931, Vol. 18 (United Provinces), Part 2.

and Faqirs flocked to it and to Islam. The number of Faqirs had grown so large by the time of Ghayasuddin Tughlaq (1320-25) that the sultan wanted to put a stop to a free treat to them and wanted them to take up some work, but his attitude was resented and the sultan maligned.[1] According to Ahmad Abbas 40, 000 beggars used to be fed by Ghayas's successor Muhammad Tughlaq.[2] Muhammad Tughlaq sometimes even attended the funeral of Faqirs.[3] The Faqirs were so well paid under Firoz Tughlaq[4] that some nobles, who used to recommend them to the liberality of the sultan, did not fail to take a 'bribe' out of their gains.[5] Generosity of kings and nobles towards Faqirs never slackened even during the Mughal period. A good number of people would have converted in medieval times to become Muslim Faqirs to form a caste in the Muslim social order in modern times.

Similar was the position with regard to the Qassab. Arab geographers of the ninth to twelfth centuries found most Indians vegetarians. Some Hindus ate hunted game but not flesh of animals and animals were not slaughtered for providing meat.[6] By many Hindus meat is still called 'shikar' (game). The Hindu Gorkhas call it only by this name. Therefore, while it could be difficult to categorically state that Hindus in the pre-Muslim period did not do the work of meat-selling, there does not seem to have been a caste of Hindu butchers which went over to Islam because of the oppression of caste system. The few Hindu butchers

1. Barani, *op. cit.*, pp.436-37.
2. Rizvi, *Tughlaq Kalin Bharat*, I, *op. cit.*, p.322. Also Ishwari Prasad, *Qaraunah Turks*, p.309.
3. *Masalik-ul-Absar*, E and D, III, p.580.
4. Barani, pp. 558-59. Afif, pp.448-49, 512.
5. Afif, p.449.
6. Al Masudi, *op. cit.*, p.19.
   Al Idrisi, *op. cit.*, p.88.
   Qazwini, *op. cit.*, p.96.

might have become Musalmans because their vocation found a flourishing and sympathetic clientele among Muhammadans but many others who were not butchers by profession would have found in cutting and selling of meat a new avenue of employment in a new society and joined it to form a Muslim caste of hundred per cent Qassab.

In the case of *darzis* or tailors, their employment chances lay more with the Muslim community. Muslims dressed elaborately,[1] and the sartorial habits of Arabs and Turks would point to even some tailors having come from abroad, and converted Hindu tailors joining their ranks. The requirements of the Sultan,[2] the elite, and even the common Muslims would have needed the services of a whole tribe of tailors, who, passing the whole day in the palace workshops or catering to the needs of the patronizing Muslim society would have found it profitable and convenient to become Muslim. The interdependence of cotton-carders, weavers, (*dhunia, julaha*) and tailors would have induced the former to embrace Islam, and once some people of this class converted to Muhammadanism, others followed suit because of class affiliation and vocational compulsions. Cotton-carders, weavers, and tailors were there both in the urban and the rural areas; only in the urban they were more skilled and produced fine quality stuffs required by the Muslim nobility and elite, and conversions seem to have occurred mostly in the urban areas; and many village *julahas* have remained Hindu. A Hajjam

1. Barani, pp.273-74.
Afif, p.263.
Also Lal, *Twilight of the Sultanate*, pp.271.
2. Ahmad Abbas says that in the royal workshops of Muhammad bin Tughlaq 200, 000 robes of honour were prepared every year for presentation to the nobles alone. In the Sultan's manufactory there were 400 silk-weavers and 500 manufacturers of golden tissues, besides others. *Masalik, op. cit.*, p.578.

does not enjoy a better status in Muslim society than a Nai in Hindu, but the Hajjam's profession provided greater avenues of economic betterment in Muslim society; he did the work of circumcision and other minor surgical operations.

Such instances need not be multiplied, but some other cases not included in the above Table may also be mentioned in passing. Many elephant drivers (*mahauts*) are today Muslims. It is on record that Muslim rulers were extremely fond of elephants. Mahmud of Ghazni had an elephant corps of 2,500 all collected from India.[1] Minhaj Siraj affirms that during Bakhtiyar's Bengal campaign, many *elephants were captured with their drivers*.[2] He also writes that Sultan Ruknuddin Firoz Shah (son of Iltutmish), "was very fond of... elephants, *and all the elephant drivers were much benefited by his bounty* (italics mine)."[3] Ferishtah says that by the time of Bahram Shah (C.E. 1240), the sultans had monopolised the privilege of keeping elephants.[4] Being in the employment of Muslim rulers and nobles, living in the palace or Sultans' forts all the time, and benefiting from their bounty, it was but profitable for them to convert to a faith in which advantages of service and profession lay. On the contrary those professional groups, which had a mixed Hindu-Muslim clientele, but whose business would have been adversely affected by losing the Hindu customers if they had converted to Islam, like the *panwaris* (betel sellers), *halwais* (sweetmeat sellers), *banias*, goldsmiths etc., did not convert and have remained Hindu through the ages.

---

1. Minhaj, *op. cit.*, p.83.
   Bosworth, *The Ghaznavids*, p.166
   S.H. Hodivala, *Studies in Indo-Muslim History* (Bombay, 1939), pp.139-40, 146.
2. *Tabqat-i-Nasiri*, trs. in E and D, II, p.315.
3. *Ibid.*, p.332.
4. Ferishtah, I, p.69.

Besides, not all low-caste Muslims have converted from low caste Hindus. Many foreign Muslims also would have been relegated to low caste on marrying low-caste women. The sultans and Amirs usually married in the families of the Rajas and Zamindars they defeated. But the common soldiers or common Musalmans would have married either in their own religious group, that is among the newly converted, or among the low-caste Hindus.[1] And as class distinctions crystallized in medieval Indian Muslim society, these people would have been given only a low caste status, having obtained it through their wives.[2] Needless to say that such Muslims, originally of foreign extraction, would have swelled the ranks of low-caste Muhammadans.

Thus the few low-caste groups which converted to Islam did so not "to escape from the tyranny of the caste system" because they have remained at as lower a rung in Muslim society as they were in Hindu, but because of new professional and vocational opportunities in a changed society. Such conversions took place mostly in urban areas. Artisans, mechanics, handicraftsmen were loyal to their guilds and their castes. Where guilds were loosely knit or contained many occupational groups, chances of conversions were more. There was a greater possibility of

1. Barbosa, *op. cit.*, I, p.74 tells how the Moplahs inter-married with low-caste natives.

2. Such was not the case only with the Muslims. All foreigners who married low-caste persons in this country were counted among low-castes. The case of the early Portuguese in India is an instance in point.

"After capturing Goa, (it became the policy of the Dominican head of the Church, and Albuquerque) at Cochin and Goa of encouraging and subsidizing marriages between native women and the Portuguese. Since most of the marriages contracted were between common Portuguese and low-caste natives.... it had the effect of lowering all Christians in the eyes of the higher castes...."

D.F. Lach, *Asia in the Making of Europe*, I, pp.230-34.

Also cf. Manucci, *op. cit.*, III, p.323 for the seventeenth century.

such a situation in the urban areas and port-towns where there was concentration of Muslim clientale and influencee of Muslim religious, political and economic leadership. In the conversions at port-towns, for example, foreign Muslim merchants played a great part. From what we know of their contribution in the conversion of South-East Asia,[1] it stands to reason that their propagandism for Islam in India too would have been very effective. The Zamorin of Calicut, for instance, encouraged the fisher-men of Malabar to become Musalmans in order to man his warships; and to this end ordered "that, in every family of fishermen in his dominions, one or more of the male members should be brought up as Muhammadans".[2] Either in deference to the wishes or specific condition of his Arab or other Muslim captains and crew, or to see that the men working on the ships under Muslims should have no caste inhibitions, the Zamorin may have issued such orders. But the fact is that today many boatmen and fishermen in Bengal and other parts of the Indian seacoast are Muhammadans. Similarly some mercantile groups like Khojas and Bohras also converted to Islam under the influence of foreign merchants, although legendary accounts attribute their conversion to saints.

Immigration

It was thus mainly converions that were responsible for the rise and growth of Muslim population in medieval India. This component of growth went on extending with Muslim territorial expansion. Immigration of foreign Muslims too helped in its growth. As has been seen at many places earlier, from the inception of Muslim rule right up to the eighteenth century foreign Muslims, especially from Persia, Central Asia and Abyssinia used to

1. D.G.E. Hall, *op. cit.*, pp.176-85.
2. Arnold, cited in Titus, p.39.

arrive in India and settle down here. Hindustan was a paradise for Muslim merchants, scholars and adventuers. Muslim regime of Hindustan promised and provided excellent jobs to all and sundry foreign Muslims. No wonder that the latter came here in large numbers to settle down and make fortunes. Hazards of journey were there no doubt,[1] but these were reduced with passing of time and minimised by migrant adventurers and merchants travelling in groups. Throughout the medieval period they came in droves, "like ants and locusts",[2] and were given here important and influenctial positions. It was naturally a one way traffic; Muslims only came, nobody migrated from here. By the seventeenth century they formed many pressure groups – like Irani and Turani – in the Mughal empire's politics and society. Many Muslims even today take pride in asserting their extra-territorial identity by adding suffixes like Iraqi and Bukhari to their names.

Polygamy

The most efficacious generator of the quick growth of Muslim population was their practice of polygamy. Marriage is enjoined on every Muslim. It is related in the Traditions that Muhammad said: "When the servant of God marries, he perfects half his religion... Consequently

---

1. Hasan Nizami, the author of *Taj-ul-Maasir* (Crown of Victories) who had come to India during the reign of Qutbuddin Aibak graphically describes in his inimitable poetical style the dangers of the journey to Hindustan. He set out from Ghazni for Delhi which to him was the "country of mercy and the altar of wealth...(but there were) the heat of the fiery blast...the wild beasts...the boughs of the jungle were so closely interlaced... A tiger was seen in every forest. In every ravine and plain poisonous serpents were met with. It came into his thoughts, will the boat of his life ever reach the shores of safety? The crow-like Hindus had intercepted the roads...You may say they were demons in human from." E and D, II, p.208.

2. For example Lal, *Twilight of the Sultanate*, p.126 for references from original sources.

in Islam, even the ascetic orders are rather married than single".[1] In Islam there is provision for temporary marriages (Mutas), multi-marriages, divorce, remarriage of widows, concubinage – in short there is freedom from all inhibitions and reservations in matters of matrimony. The insistence is on everybody marrying. Naturally celibacy is frowned upon. One of Muhammad's companions wanted to live in celibacy Muhammad "forbade him to do so".[2] According to a tradition derived from Ibn Abbas and quoted by Ibn Sa'd, popularly known as Katib al-Waqidi, the prophet's biographer, Muhammad said: "In my *ummah*, he is the best who has the largest number of wives".[3]

Practice excelled the precept. Muslim kings and commoners, nobles and soldiers, merchants and Ulema, Sufis and Qazis were all known for maintaining large or small harems according to finances and circumstances. There used to be four regular wives, and numberless concubines.[4] The result was prodigious progeny. And so the scriptures desired. Muhammad said: "Marry women who will love their husbands and be very prolific, *for I wish you to be more numerous than any other people*".[5] (italics ours). It is not surprising therefore that all Muslims ever desire to be more numerous than any other people. Polygamy, multi-marriages, etc. sometimes reached ridiculous limits so "that often the mothers of the sultan's sons could not be identified[6]," nor perhaps even the children as shown by the frantic enquiries made after the death of Alauddin, Mubarak Khalji and Muhammad bin

1. Hughes, T.P., *Dictionary of Islam*, pp. 313-314.
2. Ram Swarup, *Understanding Islam through Hadis* (New Delhi, 1983), p.57.
3. *Ibid*., p.57 n.
4. Lal, K.S., *The Mughal Harem* (New Delhi, 1988), pp.160-175.
5. Cited in Hughes, *Dictionary of Islam*, p.314.
6. M. Mujeeb, *The Indian Muslims*, p.207.

Tughlaq whether any of their sons were alive so that the throne could be offered to them. And what is true of the sultans is also true of the elite. Among Muhammadans the widows, even widows of sultans, remarried.[1] But a Hindu widow, even if she did not immolate herself, did not remarry. Sati and jauhar had a noble motivation and yet had a demographic aspect; these decimated Hindu numbers. Above all in India, as elsewhere, the growth of population is regulated to a large extent by the material condition of the people. In the medieval period the Muslims – but for the very poor sections – had better lands, more nutritious diet, and, as ruling classes everywhere, were in happier circustances.

Higher Fecundity

In the Hindu-Muslim mixed marriages the couple and the progeny invariably became Muslim. This practice formed another important component of growth of Muslim population in India. There is also higher fecundity among Muslims. Kingsley Davis rightly remarks that "in six decades (1881-1941)... at no census have the Muslims failed to improve their percentage and the Hindus failed to lose..." It is due not only to the "proportion of Muslim women married, but those who are married also have a higher fertility."[2] Today every seventh man in the world is a Muslim,[3] and in this great rise of Muslim population their high fertility should have contributed its share. Dudley Kirk, after a detailed study of fertility among various nationalities and religious groups, too, has arrived

1. "The Sultan's (Bahram Shah, son of Iltutmish) sister had been married to Kazi Nasiruddin, but being widowed, the deputy took her to wife." Sultan Nasiruddin's widowed mother was married to Katlagh Khan, Minhaj, E and D, II, pp.338, 354 respectively.
2. Davis, *op. cit.*, p.193.
3. H.W. Hazard, *Atlas of Islamic History* (Princeton, 1954), p.5.

at the conclusion that birth rate among Muslims is the highest.[1]

Lesser Losses

While Muslim population rose through conversion, immigration, and polygamy, and possibly high rate of fertility, its losses in wars and famines were lesser than those of the Hindus, and its natural growth was high.

We have referred at many places to the losses of Muslims in war. But a major portion of Muslim armies consisted of Hindus. Even Mahmud of Gazni's forces had Hindu contigents. During the Sultanate period Muslims, especially foreign Muslims, belonged to the officer cadre and were mostly cavalrymen; Hindus are often mentioned as Paiks or footsoldiers. The Paiks formed the rank and file and probably the bulk of the Muslim armies. There were large armies in India, both in the North and the South, of Bahmani, Vijayanagar, Mughal. The second volume of Abul Fazl's *Ain-i-Akbari* gives lists of the large number of Hindu contingents that could be called to duty under Akbar. Naturally it is these who were killed in large numbers in wars being placed, as infantry was then

---

1. Kirk needs to be quoted at length :

"1. Islamic countries uniformly have high birth rates.

2. These are supported by distinctive Islamic attitudes and practices in family life rather than by political or religious doctrine.

3. The 'normal' diffusion of birth control to and within Muslim countries on the European pattern has been inhibited by the cultural discontinuity between Muslim peoples and their neighbours.

4. The continuing high birth rates in Muslim countries, matched with increasing progress in reducing deaths, now lead to rapid population growth and its especially high visibility as a handicap to economic and social progress."

Dudley Kirk "Factors Affecting Moslem Natality" in Olivia Schieffelin (Ed.) *Muslim Attitudes Towards Family Planning,* Demographic Division, The Population Council, Inc. (New York, 1967), p.79.

placed, in a vulnerable position.[1] The Hindus thus died not only for defending their kings and kingdoms during the unending process of Muslims territorial expansion; they also died in large numbers for their Muslim masters as soldiers in the latter's armies.[2] Compared with theirs, the loss of the Muslim numbers was small. Muslim population at least was not affected by these wars, because any loss in battles was more than made up by the number of captives, who used to be converted and also by replenishment through immigration.

Whenever famines occurred Muslim rulers took necessary steps to provide relief to the people. But from the narative of the chroniclers it is evident that these relief measures were mostly confined to urban areas. And Muslims were mostly concentrated in urban areas. Even in the cities sometimes the mission of mercy was marred by bigotry. "Between 1387 and 1395 the Deccan was visited

---

1. al-Qalqashindi, describing the battle array of Muhammad bin Tughlaq clearly brings this point home. He says, "according to Sirajuddin -al-Hindi... the Sultan stands in the centre (of the army)...the archers stand before and behind him...In front of him are the elephants. In front of the elephants march the slaves in light dress wearing shields and weapons. They hold the ropes of the elephants while the horsemen are to their right and left...*so that not one of them can run away*" (Italics mine). *Subh-ul-Asha*, p.76.
2. An interesting incident during the Battle of Haldighati bears out this statement. Akbar sent Raja Man Sing and Asaf Khan against Rana Pratap of Mewar in 1576. There were Rajput soldiers on both sides; those under Rana Pratap were fighting the ones under Raja Man Singh. At one stage in the fierce struggle, Badaoni asked Asaf Khan how he could distinguish between the friendly and the enemy Rajputs. Asaf Khan replied: "Shoot at whomsoever you like, on whichever side they may be killed, it will be a gain to Islam."
Smith, *Akbar the Great Mogul*, pp.108-109.
Lal, *Studies in Medieval Indian Hisotry*, pp.171-172.

by a severe famine, and Muhammad's[1] measures for the relief of his subjects displayed a combination of administrative ability, enlightened compassion, and religious bigotry. A thousand bullocks belonging to the transport establishement maintained for the court were placed at the disposal of those in charge of relief measures, and travelled incessantly to and fro between his dominions and Gujarat and Malwa, which had escaped the visitation, bringing thence grain which was sold at low rates in the Deccan, but to Muslims only.".[2] And Muhammad Bahmani was not the only orthodox sultan in medieval India. It may not be proper to generalize, but probably in famines and such like calamities the Muslims suffered less loss than the Hindus.

1. Ferishtah, I, p.302 says that the correct name of the sultan is Muhammad and not Mahmud. He also writes that relief measures were undertaken in "large cities and *qasbas* " like Gulbarga, Bidar, Khandahar, Ellichpur etc.
2. C.H.I., III, p.385.

Chapter 6

Factors which Checked Islamization of India

Now, if the components of growth of Muslim population were many, Muslim losses comparatively few, and fecundity among them high, the problem that needs investigation is why Muslims have remained a minority in this country and why India, unlike many other countries in the medieval period, could not be completely converted to Islam.

Vastness of the Country

The vastness of the country and its natural and political division into regions and kingdoms made the task of its complete subjugation and conversion extremely difficult. In fact throughout the medieval period at no time was the whole of India under direct Muslim rule. Even in the regions where Muslim rule was firmly established it was thought expedient to leave the countryside alone. Victories provided the Muslim ruling class the luxuries of the city cultured life, and their interest in rural areas remained confined merely to the collection of land revenue. In the words of Kingsley Davis, "although there were mass conversions, the country was too vast, the invaders too few, and the volume of immigration too small to change the social complex...India, therefore, never became a Muslim nation, but remained simply a Hindu country in which Muslims were numerous".[1] Henry Blochmann puts it more explicitly. He writes: "The invaders were few and the country was too large and too populous.

1. Davis, *op. cit.*, p.191.

The waves of immigration from Turan were few and far between, and deposited on Indian soil adventurers, warriors, and learned men, rather than artisans and colonists. Hence the Muhammadans depended upon the Hindoos for labour of every kind, from architecture down to agriculture and the supply of servants. Many branches they had to learn from the Hindoos, as, for example, the cultivation of indigeneous produce, irrigation, coinage, medicine, the building of houses, and weaving of stuffs suitable for the climate, the management of elephants, and so forth."[1]

Hindu 'Protestant' Movement

Another reason for India remaining a Hindu majority country was the resistance of the people to conversion to Islam. Before the advent of Islam India had seen the birth and growth of many religions and sects like Shaivism, Vaishnavism, Jainism, Buddhism, Shankara's neo-Hinduism, etc. People had freely 'converted', 'reconverted' and at times conformed to more than one religious belief at one and the same time. For all this was a matter of conviction brought about by peaceful methods.

But the Hindus could not have liked being converted by conquerors and rulers by force. In fact, as seen in Sind after the return of Muhammad bin Qasim and in Karnataka after the death of Tipu Sultan, many Hindus, who were converted to Islam, returned to their former faith on the first opportunity. Harihar and Bukka, converted to Islam by Muhammad bin Tughlaq, reverted to Hinduism and founded the kingdom of Vijayanagar to resist the expansion of Muslim power in the South. Although any return of converts to the Hindu fold was frowned upon by the Muslim rulers, and some Brahmins

1. Blochmann, "A Chapter from Muhammadan History" in *The Calcutta Review*, No. civ. 1871 cited in Bernier, p.40 n.

encouraging converts to return to Hinduism were put to death by Firoz Tughlaq and Sikandar Lodi,[1] yet there did exist some mechanism which facilitated return of converted Hindus back into their old religion. Else, with what actually happened in medieval times, Hindus would have been completely submerged under the onslaught of unmitigated proselytization. The Hindus did not believe in converting others to their faith, but the tenacity of the Hindu social order "lapped away at any instrusive system as the sea laps away at a sand bank".[2] Yet in the fourteenth and fifteenth centuries in particular there were conversions on such large scale throughout the country, that for once "the bleeding soul of the Hindus" rose in revolt.[3] The Bhakti saints were the leaders of the Hindu 'protestant' movement.[4]

It must be said at the outset that there is no recorded evidence to show that the Bhakti saints of the fifteenth century made any *deliberate* attempt to put a stop to conversions to Islam, or to reconvert people to Hinduism. Still there is good deal of circumstantial evidence to show that their reform movement did help check Muslim proselytizing activity. It is significant that the socio-religious reformers associated with the Bhakti movement of the fifteenth century were all Hindus. There is some doubt about Kabir's parentage, but then,"the whole background of Kabir's thought is Hindu".[5] Indeed

1. Afif, *op. cit.*, pp. 379-81. Dorn, *Makhzan-i-Afghani*, (London, 1829), pp.65-66. Ferishtah, *op. cit.*, I, p.182. Also Lal, *Twilight, op. cit.*, p.191.
2. K. Davis, *op. cit.*, p.195.
3. *Indian Heritage*, Bharatiya Vidya Bhavan, Vol. I (Bombay, 1955), p.227.
4. Kabir declared : "I have come to save the devotees. I was sent here because the world was seen in misery." Tara Chand, *op. cit.*, pp.150-151.
5. G.H. Westcott, *Kabir and the Kabir Panth* (Cawnpore, 1907), p.118. "The contrast," observesAhmad Shah, "of Kabir's intimate Hindu thought, writings and ritual with the purely superficial knowledge of Moslem belief revealed in the Bijak is too striking to be ignored." Ahmad Shah, *Bijak of Kabir* (Hamirpur, 1917), p.40.

Kamal, the son of Kabir, who "probably had greater leaning towards Islamic ways of thinking", is remembered in the *Adigrantha* by the disparaging line: "the family of Kabir foundered when Kamal the son was born".[1]

A striking feature of the Bhakti movement was that it gave to the backward class Hindus a respectable position in the society. Indeed some of the leaders of this movement like Sain, Raidas, and Dhanna belonged to the lowest classes of Hindu social order. Because of this 'revolution' in which the lowest classes of people, even the untouchables, had not only got an equal status with the highest, but were even revered as saints,[2] there could have been no incentive for the low classes of people to renounce their faith, if they ever had any before "because of Hindu tyranny," and go over to Islam. As Aziz Ahmad puts it, "like other Bhakti poets his (Kabir's) denunciation of the caste-system was as much an inspiration of Muslim example as a response to its pull of conversion."[3] When Kabir denounced caste and ritual of the Hindus, he also denounced the superstitions and rituals of the Muslims: or, conversely, the idea is best expressed in the words of his disciple Naudhan (whom Sikandar Lodi executed): Islam was true, but his own religion was also true.[4] This was an open challenge to Muslim propagandism and proselytization. No wonder that Bhakti reformers were disliked by some Sufi Mashaikh, who looked upon them as competitors.[5] For, under the influence of these saints many Muslims were converted to Bhakti Hinduism. Namdeva,[6] Ramdas,

1 Tara Chand, *op. cit.*, pp.182, 185.
2. Ibid, pp.179, 181.
3. Aziz Ahmad, *op. cit.*, p.146.
4. Dorn, *History of the Afghans*, I, 65; Ferishtah, I, 182.
5. S.A.A. Rizvi, *op. cit.*, pp.57-58.
6. M.G. Ranade, *Rise of the Maratha Power* (Publications Division, Delhi, 1961), p.75.

Eknath, Ramanand, Kabir, Nanak and Chaitanya and several other saints had Muslim disciples, many of whom converted to the Hindu Bhakti cult. Chaitanya openly converted Muslims to Bhakti Hinduism.[1] The *Bhaktamala* relates many instances of conversions that Pipa effected.

The effects of the mission of the socio-religious reformers with regard to conversion of people to Hinduism were significant. They themselves had adhered to peaceful methods but not their followers in later years. Kabir's disciples spread out throughout North India and the Deccan. Jiwan Das was the founder of the Satnami sect which took up arms against the Mughals. The Sikh disciples of Nanak's successor Gurus, for varied reasons, fought against the Mughals and many times converted people by force. So did the Marathas. Manucci and Khafi Khan both affirm that the Marathas used to capture Muslim women "because (adds Manucci) the Mahomedans had interfered with Hindu women in (their) territories."[2] Chaitanya's influence in Bengal as of Nanak in the Punjab is still great. According to Abdul Majid Khan it is because of Chaitanya's influence that large-scale conversions to Hinduism took place at the end of the eighteenth and beginning of nineteenth century.[3]

Thus whether it was their motive or mission or not, the work of the Bhakti reformers helped in checking conversions to Islam and reclaiming many converted Hindus back to their former faith.

---

1. D.C. Sen, *Chaitanya and His Age* (Calcutta, 1922), p.14. Abdul Karim, *op. cit., Social History of the Muslims in Bengal*, pp.150, 202-204.
M.T. Kennedy, *The Chaitanya Movement* (Calcutta, 1925), p.213. Tara Chand, *op. cit.*, p.219.
D.C. Sen, *History of Bengali Literature*, pp.228-29.
Indian Heritage, op. cit., I. p.249.
2. Manucci, *op. cit.* ,II, p.119.
Khafi Khan, *op. cit.*, II, pp.115-18.
3. Abdul Majid Khan, *Research about Muslim Aristocracy, op. cit.*, pp.23-25.

Caste System

The Caste System also contributed its mite to the preservation of Hindu social order, indirectly checking proselytization. Some modern writers think that it was the degraded status of low caste Hindus and the social democracy of Islam that were responsible for large-scale conversions to Muhammadanism in medieval times. Many others give the caste system all the credit for saving India from becoming Islamised.

But neither caste was so oppressive nor Muslim society so democratic. Within the framework of the caste system some sort of vertical and horizontal mobility was always permitted. There was also a sense of pride in belonging to one's caste whether high or low. However, for any error caste did not fail to punish, and sometimes even ostracized the delinquent whether or not the act of omission or commission was due to his own fault. In a few such cases conversion was a welcome way out. Therefore some conversions would have taken place because of the rigid caste rules although contemporary accounts are silent on this point. On the contrary this very rigidity served as a bulwark against proselytization and to this contemporary accounts bear witness. To the majority caste was synonymous with religion, and so there was a general reluctance and often resistance to conversion to Islam both by the high and the low caste Hindus.

Let us study the case of the lowest classes first. Alberuni writes at length on the caste system. About the lowest castes, or the so low as to be casteless, he has this to say:

"After the Sudra follow the people called *Antyaja,* who render various kinds of services, who are not reckoned amongst any caste, but only as members of certain craft or profession. There are eight classes of them, who freely intermarry with each other, except the fuller, shoemaker, and weaver, for no others would condescend to have anything to do with them. These eight guilds are the fuller, shoemaker, juggler, the basket and shield maker, the sailor, the fisherman, the hunter of wild animals and of birds, and the weaver ...... These guilds live near the villages and towns.........but outside them.

"The people called Hadi, Doma (Domba), Candala, and Badhatau (*sic*) are not reckoned amongst any caste or guild. They are occupied with dirty work, like the cleaning of the villages and other services. They are considered one sole class, and distinguished only by their occupations...They are considered like illegitimate children.......they are degraded outcastes...

"Of the classes beneath the castes, the Hadi are the best spoken of, because they keep themselves from everything unclean......the Doma...play on the flute and sing. The still lower classes practice as a trade killing and the inflicting of judicial punishments..."[1]

Vis-a-vis Alberuni's list of backward castes in the medieval period, is the Table[2] of backward castes in modern times prepared on the basis of U.P. Census Report of 1931:

The Table clearly shows that most of the lowest castes included in Alberuni's list from Chamar downwards have not only continued to remain Hindu, but, even their caste subdivisions have multiplied. Alberuni has been quoted at length, not because his study of the caste-structure in India is precise, but because he provides the clue to the non-conversion of low caste Hindus to Islam. His notice shows that (a) the caste-system denied equality to the low classes, (b) that it was based on craft or profession, and (c) that it was hierarchical.

1. Alberuni, *op. cit.*, I, pp.101-102.
2. Complied from the Census Report of India, 1931, Vol.18 (United Provinces), Part 2.

Table

Showing some Hindu low Castes of U.P.

	Per cent of caste Members adhering to Hindu Religion	Per cent of each caste in Total Religious Membership
Chamar	99.7	15.1
Ahir	97.7	9.4
Kurmi	99.7	4.2
Pasi	100.0	3.5
Kahar	99.1	2.8
Lodh	99.7	2.6
Gadariya	99.6	2.4
Kori	99.9	2.2
Kumhar	98.7	1.9
Teli	74.8	1.8
Kachi	99.9	1.7

Caste-system was bad, but it had two redeeming features. One was that since the low classes were 'distinguished only by their occupations' and they intermarried, there was occupational and vocational mobility and also perhaps some sort of social Sanskritization. Another is that it had (and has) an hierchical structure, and even low caste people feel proud of being superior to some other lower castes. Thus a Teli feels himself superior to an Ahir, an Ahir to a Chamar, a Kahar to a Pasi, and so on. In Bengal, the land of mass conversions, caste pride among low caste Hindus was as pronounced as elsewhere. About the Dom, sometimes also called Chandala, H.H. Risley says that he will eat the leavings of others, but "no Dom will touch the leavings of a Dhobi, nor will he take water...or any sort of food or drink from a man of that caste... Pods or Chasi, a fishing, cultivating and land-holding caste of lower Bengal will eat the leavings of Brahman, but Vaishnava Pods abstain from all kinds of flesh. Rajbansi, a synonym for Koch, wear sacred thread in Bihar."[1]

In fact the lower class people are more particular about 'caste preservation' than even the higher caste ones, and "the Hadi... keep themselves free from everything unclean." A significant point to note is that even the lowest classes had an importance of their own in Hindu society. In Hindu marriage, for example, the cooperation and services of Nai, Dhobi, Kumhar, Kahar etc. were and are as important as that of the Brahmin Purohit. The higher castes depended as much on the lower as the lower on the higher. All castes and non-castes were an essential part of the Hindu social and economic order. Therefore, and in spite of the discrimination, low caste people have been as unwilling to convert as the high. That is how most of Alberuni's *Antyaja*, as the Census Table above shows, have not converted – the fuller (Dhobi), shoemaker (Chamar),

1. H.H. Risley. *The Tribes and Castes of Bengal*, Bengal Secretariat Press, (Calcutta, 1891).

Juggler (Nat), Fisherman (Kachhi, Macchua), hunters and bird catchers (Gadariya), Doma (basket-maker, street dancer, singer). That there are, about 60 million 'untouchable' Hindus to-day is the greatest proof of their ancestors' unwillingness to convert in medieval times.

There is also recorded contemporary evidence of the unwillingness of the backward people to voluntarily convert to Islam. Mahmud of Ghazni used to convert people by force, but his contemporary Alberuni (eleventh century) nowhere mentions voluntary conversions of Hindus. Writing about the backward class Hindus called Govis (now called Paraiyar) Marco Polo (thirteenth century) says: "Nothing on earth would induce them to enter the place where Messer St. Thomas is – I mean where his body lies...Indeed, were even twenty or thirty men to lay hold of these Govis and to try to hold them in the place where the Body of the Blessed Apostle of Jesus Christ lies buried they could not do it."[1] This is the testimony about the South. About North, Shaikh Nizamuddin Auliya (fourteenth century) at many places admits that Hindus "do not embrace Islam", and that "the heart of these people is not changed through sermons".[2] In the seventeenth century Manucci wrote that the backward caste people were proud of their caste and were reluctant to convert.[3] Caste gave them freedom and dignity of the kind which no other system did.

In short, contemporary evidence does not speak of low caste as a factor contributing to conversions to Islam. The presence of a large number of vocational groups among Muslims is due to the fact, mentioned earlier, that Muslim regime and society provided people with new

1. H. Yule and H. Cordier, *Ser Marco Polo*, 2 vols. (New York, 1903), II, p.341.
2. Amir Hasan Sijzi, *Fawaid-ul-Fuad* (Delhi, 1865), pp. 150, 195-97.
3. Manucci, *op. cit.*, III, p.173. Also II, p.238.

avenues of employment. Those who lacked resources of self-defence during war or those who could not make both ends meet without a change of religion, converted. Among these surely the people of low caste predominated. But caste system as such had little to contribute to conversions.

Conversions of high caste Hindus were also few. Hindu religion and philosophy were ancient, vast and deep, and Hindu intellectuals, intelligentia and high castes were proud, as Alberuni points out, of a highly developed philosophy of their own. He writes that "The Hindus believe that there is no country but theirs, no nation like theirs, no king like theirs, no religion like theirs, no science like theirs."[1] It was no easy matter to induce such people to convert.[2] It is true that prospects of employment under Muslim government would have provided some incentive for conversion even to high caste people, and a few instances of conversion for aquiring economic and status benefits are on record.[3] But in the early medieval period job opportunities being limited and high offices being monopolised by Turks or Muslims of foreign extraction, infiltration of and competition by Hindu converts in government service was resented. Cases of Imad-ud-din Rahyan, Nasiruddin Khusrau and Ain-ul-Mulk Multani are instances in point. They are referred to with contempt by the Turkish ruling class. Minhaj Jurjani asserts, rather bluntly, that "Turks of pure lineage and Tajiks of noble

---

1. Alberuni, I, p.22.
2. See the way of Raja Man Singh's refusal to convert in M.Mujeeb, *op. cit.* p.360.
3. Sadharan of Thaneshwar married his sister to Firoz Tughlaq, accompanied him to Delhi, and later became Wajahat-ul-Mulk (distinguished man of the State).
Sikandar bin Muhammad, *Mirat-i-Sikandari* (Bombay, 1308 H), pp.5-8. Also S.C.Misra, *Rise of Muslim Power in Gujarat*, pp.137-39, and Mahdi Husain, *Tughlaq Dynasty*, p.408.

birth could not tolerate (Imad-ud-din of)...the tribes of Hind to rule over them".[1] Thus the attitude of the foreign-extraction Muslims repeatedly expressed in the diatribe of Muslim chroniclers who usually call them "low born" would have discouraged Hindus to convert even for the allurement of jobs.

In the Mughal period Hindus began to be appointed to high posts but for getting these there was no need to convert. Power sharing by the Mughals was not due to liberal Islam. It was prompted by exigencies of the situation, and in the power-equation conversion stood ruled out. Manucci states that under Aurangzeb three Rajas embraced Islam against promises and temptations offered by the emperor, but later they regretted their conversion and remained unhappy[2] because Hindu converts to Islam commanded little respect.[3] Needless to add that lower Hindu castes could not get equality with the other Muslims in the "democratic" Muslim social order. They carried their caste and social status with them even after their conversion and high class Muslims would not mix or even eat with them if modern practices are any indication for the medieval.[4]

From the modern census figures it appears that not many high caste people voluntarily converted to Islam in medieval times. Bohras, Khojas, Ismailis and Mopilahs were, by and large, converted by peaceful methods from high caste Hindus except perhaps the Mopilahs. But their statistics in modern times show how small their numbers would have been in medieval. According to the census of

1. Minhaj, Raverty, *op. cit.*, p .829
2. Manucci, *op. cit.*, II, p.436.
3. *Ibid.*, p.451.
4. A.K. Nazmul Karim, "Muslim Social Classes in East Pakistan", *op. cit.*, pp.120-130, 138-143.
Also E.A. Gait, *Census of India Report*, 1901, VI, pp.439-442, and *Ibid*. II, p.544.

1921 there were about 5 million Shias; a little over one million Mopilahs; 382,000 Labbes; 153,363 Bohras; and 146,000 Khojas in India (now India and Pakistan).[1] Keeping in view the patronage Persian officers had in Muslim courts in India, it is certain that a good number would have come from outside in the medieval period. But even with local converts and with centuries of growth in numbers their small figures in modern times point only to a few voluntary conversions in medieval times. The 1931 Census Report of U.P. presents the following picture of Muslim and Hindu high castes.[2]

Table
Showing High Castes of Hindus and Muslims

Castes	Per cent of Caste Members	Per cent of Total Religious Membership falling in each caste.
Muslim Castes		
Shaikh	100.0	?
Saiyyad	100.0	4.2
Mughal	100.0	0.8
Pathan	100.0	21.4
Rajputs	4.4	2.2
Hindu Castes		
Brahman	99.4	10.9
Rajput	94.2	8.5
Vaishya	92.7	2.8

1. Also Titus, *op. cit.*, pp.40, 41, 87, 99, 103, 106.
2. Adopted from the Table prepared by Kingsley Davis, *op. cit.*, p.165, complied from Census of India Report, 1931, Vol.18 (United Provinces), part 2.

It is probable that not all high caste Muslims are of foreign extraction, but the percentage of high caste Hindus clearly indicates that their ancestors were disinclined to convert in medieval times so as to bring out the above picture in modern times.

Akbar's Regulations

It has been seen in the earlier chapter that the largest number of converts were obtained during wars through enslavement. Many people embraced Islam to escape death; and captive women and children "used to be converted to Islam".[1] But early in his reign (1562) The Mughal emperor Akbar (1556-1605) abolished the custom of enslaveing helpless people in times of war.[2] These humanitarian but revolutionary steps would have put a check on large-scale conversions. Akbar did not give any economic inducements for conversion. On the contrary he removed all modes of economic pressure which sometimes led to conversions. He abolished the Jiziyah in 1564. Firoz Tughlaq is witness to the fact that its strict enforcement brought many converts to Islam. Akbar was determined to see this tax go, and probably finding that it still lingered in some places issued, in 1579, another declaration reiterating its abolition.[3] Earlier in 1563 he had abolished the Pilgrim Tax on the Hindus.[4]

---

1. S.R. Sharma, *The Religious Policy of the Mughal Emperors,* p.21.
2. Du Jarric, *Akbar and the Jesuits*, pp.152-59. Oral orders for the abolition of this practice were given much earlier.
See Du Jarric, pp.28, 30, 67, 70, 87, 92.
3. R.P. Tripathi, *Some Aspects of Muslim Administration,* p.318.
4. *Akbar Nama,* II, p.190.
Smith, *op. cit.,* pp.47-48.

Thus in Akbar's time, because of the above mentioned and several other similar measures, conversions to Islam by force, through enslavement, or economic pressure, seem to have been restricted. Even the Mullas and Mashaikh could not have received any encouragement from the government for the work of proselytization. The hope "of obtaining *mawajib* and *ghanaim*" (rewards and booty) was perhaps still there, but for this conversion was not necessary as posts were thrown open to all without prejudice to religion or creed. Besides the effect on Muslim numbers of the conversions that might still have taken place, was offset by Akbar's order permitting such Hindus as had been forcibly converted to Islam to reconvert to their original faith.[1] All restrictions on Hindu worship and building of temples were also lifted.[2] Although contemporary accounts are silent as to the numbers that went back to Hinduism as a result of this permission; yet the facts that Jahangir severely punished those who adopted Hinduism of their own free will, Shahjahan once again made apostasy from Islam a capital crime, and Aurangzeb did his best at Muslim proselytization, show that people were taking advantage of Akbar's order. Probably Akbar had only removed obstructions in a practice which was probably always prevalent, but his measures removed pressure on the Hindus to embrace Islam. Obviously conversions should have become rather scarce.

1. Badaoni, *op. cit.*, II,317.
2. Du Jarric. *op. cit.*, p.75.

Christian Missionaries

The arrival of Christian missionaries also helped check Muslim proselytization. Vasco da Gama landed in India in 1498. In 1510 the Portuguese captured Goa, in 1531 Diu, and in 1534 Daman. In the triumphal entry into Goa, "the clergymen were at the head of the procession."[1] Muslim proselytizting activity not only received a check but a challenge at the hands of these Christian missionaries.

It is exceedingly interesting to note that the agencies of conversion to the Semetic religions, Islam and Christianity, were, the same – inter-communal marriages, force and enslavement, and missionary endeavour. Portuguese missionary activity was well organised and quite effective. In Goa, Albuquerque encouraged his soldiers to marry in the families of Turkish officers.[2] To promote mixed marriages, Portuguese with Indian wives as well as neoconverts, were treated as a privileged class for appointment to petty offices.[3] Force was also openly used for obtaining converts.[4] "In 1560, the year the Inquisition was set up, 13,092 Hindus were forcibly converted. In 1578, the...missionaries pulled down 350 temples and converted 100,000 people."[5] Similar, and in some cases worse, treatment was meted out to Muhammadans. Consequently by 1583 Goa had by and large become Christian, while Salsette had a Christian population of 8,000. After Goa, Cochin was the next Mission Centre. By 1570 there were more than twentyfive Christain stations in Travancore and about 15,000 converts. In 1600 Mission Centres in Travancore had risen to fifty. Converts on the

1. R.P. Rao, *Portuguese Rule in Goa*, p.34.
2. T.B. Cunha, *Goa's Freedom Struggle*, p.11.
3. Rao, *op. cit.*, p.31.
4. *Ibid.*, p.42.
5. *Ibid.*, p.44.

Fishery Coast alone are estimated from 90,000 to 130,000.[1] Christian Missions made successful efforts in converting low caste people. Appreciative of the attitude of the Indian people, Henrique advised Loyola: "It is better in India to baptize all those of one caste than different individuals taken from various castes".[2]

In times of famine they bought children, and even men and women, and sold them at high prices, but "Portuguese under pain of severe punishments, are forbidden to sell heathen slaves to Muslims, since heathens are converted more easily to Christianity under Portuguese and to Islam under Muslim ownership."[3]

The capture of Goa by the Portuguese was facilitated by Hindu cooperation. Some Hindu chiefs of Goa invited Albuquerque to help them relieve "the Hindu population from the fanatical oppression of Adil Shah's governor at Goa."[4] In the Vijayanagar empire relations were generally good between Hindus and Christians, who were united if for no other reason, by the common hostility to Muslim.[5] All this facilitated Christian missionary activity in the South. In the North, the Mughal Emperor Akbar invited Portuguese missions and permitted Jesuit Fathers to convert people to Christianity. They had their Mission Centres in as important places as Lahore, Delhi, and Agra.[6]

It hardly need be asserted that wherever the Portuguese went, the Muslim proselytizing endeavour received a severe blow. Muslim numbers even were depleted. Barbosa gives a graphic account of Rander in

1. Lach, *Asia in the Making of Europe*, I, pp.264, 265, 271.
2. Henrique to Loyola from Bombay, October 31, 1548. J. Wicki (ed.) *Documenta Indica* (Rome, 1960), III, p.599, cited in Lach, I, p.443.
3. Lach, I, pp.239, 487.
4. Rao, *op. cit.*, p.29.
5. Lach, *op. cit.*, I, p.370, on the authority of Danvers.
6. Smith, *op. cit.*, pp.189-190, 209-210.

Gujarat with its rich Muslim merchants, their high style of living, and their richly decorated mansions. Danvers narrates its destruction by the Portuguese. Muslim trade and population were so adversely affected by arrival of the Portuguese that Barbosa laconically comments: "Now (the Muslims that) there are do not live independently."[1] What Barbosa says about Malabar, may be said about India as a whole. Barbosa contends that the coming of Portuguese alone prevented Malabar from becoming a Moorish state.[2] It may as well be said that the coming of European nations and the establishment of British rule prevented India from becoming a Muslim land.

Muslim Cult of Violence

It was not only because of Hindu and Christian attitudes and actions that rise of Muslim population received a check; aggression and violence which was their natural trait even remained directed against themselves too. Of the ten Sultans of the so-called Slave Dynasty (1206-1290), at least six were deposed, poisoned or murdered. In each such case many Muslim lives were lost. Many dynasties changed during the Sultanate period. With every change of dynasty, scions of Muslim royalty, nobility and commoners were killed with abandon. The Khalji royal family was completely liquidated in 1320. The princes and slaves of the Tughlaqs were systematically massacred after the death of Firoz Tughlaq in 1388. Sword was the ultimate arbiter in Muslim political life. Writing about the warfare among the states into which Bahmani kingdom had been divided, Nuniz says: "There is little faith among the Moors and they bite one another like

1. Barbosa, *op. cit.*, II, p.78.
2. *Ibid.*, p.74.

dogs, and like to see one after the other destroyed".[1] Mughal princes rebelled and more often than not fought pitched battles with parents. Shahjahan waded through blood to the throne. Aurangzeb killed all his brothers with great loss of Muslim lives. After his death in 1707, centrifugal forces were let loose in northern India. The Mughal princes got busy in wars of succession, and in one battle alone, fought between Shah Alam and Azam Tara, "one hundred and eighty thousand horsemen lay dead", without speaking of the "infantry or the elephants".[2] Too much violence and aggressiveness on the part of the Muslims turned out to be a death-wish. As if killings among themselves were not enough, they invited the enmity of Jats, Sikhs and Marathas which resulted in great Muslim losses. They all directed their wrath against Delhi "It is significant that the chief gateway of every Maratha fortress is Delhi Gate."[3] Nadir Shah and Ahmad Shah Abdali killed their co-religionists without compunction.

The surest evidence of the decline of Muslim population in the eighteenth century is to be found in the decline of the three Capitals of the Muslim empire – Lahore, Delhi and Agra.

Lahore was ever very populous. Monserrate and Finch had written about its large population late in the sixteenth century. According to Sujan Rai in the time of Shahjahan its population increased daily.[4] To Bernier Delhi (in 1663) was as great as Paris in beauty, extent and inhabitants.[5] Sujan Rai enumerates people of almost

---

1. Cited in Robert Sewell, *A Forgotten Empire,* Publication Division (Delhi, 1962), p.326.
Also H.K. Sherwani, *The Bahamanis of the Deccan* (Hyderabad, n.d.) p.51.
2. Manucci, *op. cit.*, IV, p.403.
3. C.H.I. IV, p.397.
4. Sujan Rai, *Khulasat-ul-Tawarikh,* ed. Zafar Hasan (Delhi, 1918), p.81. Also Thevenot, *Indian Travels of Thevenot and Careri,* ed. S.N. Sen, (New Delhi, 1949).p.85, and Manucci, *op. cit* , II, p.186.
5. Bernier, *op. cit.*, p.282.

all nationalities as living in Delhi.[1] Fatehpur Sikri had been gradually abandoned after 1585 and most of its inhabitants seem to have shifted to Agra, so that Coryat (1612-17) found it larger than Rome. Manrique, who visited Agra in 1640, estimated its population at 660,000 inhabitants, "besides the large number of strangers who continually fill ninety caravansarais and other private houses."[2] Thus the population of Agra rose from over two lacs at the close of the sixteenth century to about seven lacs by the middle of the seventeenth century. And this was the position after the plague of 1616-24 had earlier devastated the city. In the seventeenth century the population of Sikri-Agra-Sikandara had probably touched the million mark.[3]

But internal wars and external invasions, had a devastating effect on Muslim population. W. Francklin, who travelled through the major parts of northern India between 1793 and 1796,[4] and wrote an eye-witness account of Delhi, says that ever since the massacre of Nadir Shah, Delhi was "but very thinly populated." About the close of the eighteenth century, when he wrote, "the Bazars of Delhi are at present but indifferently furnished, and the population of late years miserably reduced."[5] The population of the cities of the Punjab was decimated by

---

1. *Khulasat-ul-Tawarikh, op. cit.*, p.5.
2. Manrique, *op. cit.*, II, p.151.
3. In comparison the population of London in 1593-95 was 152, 479 and in 1666, 460, 000 (*Ency. Brit.* XI Ed., XVI, p.965). The population of Paris in 1590 has been estimated at 200, 000 and under Louis XIV (d. 1715) at 492, 600 (*Modern Cyclopaedia* , London, 1901, VI, p.305.).Shahajahan probably transferred the capital to Delhi from Agra (1649) because of too much congestion in th latter. *Arch. Sur. Rep.* 1911-12, p.2, and contemporary authorities cited therein.
4. W. Francklin, *The History of the Reign of the Shah-Aulum,* (Allahabad, 1915: First published 1798), Preface, p.i.
5. *Ibid.*, pp.199-200.

the invasions of Abdali. No wonder that in the eighteenth century no foreign or Indian writer compares the population of prestigious Muslim cities with those of London, Paris, Rome, Constantinople or Cairo.

Epilogue

We began by noting that the sword of Islam was blunted in India. Islam had spread in Arabia, Syria, Egypt, Iran, Iraq, North Africa and even parts of Europe with a bang. Within a hundred years of the death of the Prophet this spectacular success had been achieved through the instrument of *Jihad*. It appeared as if there was no stopping the Islamic avalanche on the Globe, both to the east and the the west of the land of its birth – Arabia. But contrary to all hopes and expectations, Islam received a check in a most unexpected quarter – Hindustan, a country believed to be divided by caste, torn by dissensions and indifferent to conventionality in religious faith. Persistent efforts were made to Islamize India but to no avail.

At various points of time it was fervently hoped by Muslims that all the Hindus would be converted to Islam. The Arab invasion of Sind saw lot of proselytization, but such conversions proved to be temporary. "The tide of Islam, having overflowed Sind and the lower Punjab, ebbed, leaving (only) some jetsam on the strand."[1] Three hundred years later Mahmud of Ghazni's exertions raised fresh hopes. He promised the Khalifa that he would convert the country through his yearly expeditions. He did his worst. In the words of Alberuni, "Mahmud utterly ruined the prosperity of the country, by which the Hindus became like atoms of dust scattered in all directions, and like a tale of old in the mouth of the people."[2] But no, the Hindus did not become a tale of old. They remained

1. Wolseley Haig, *Cam. Hist. India*, III, p.10.
2. Alberuni's *India*, p.22.

entrenched in their country, so that when Timur invaded India at the end of the fourteenth century, the inhabitants of India were found by him to be cheifly "polytheists and infidels". "My principal object in the invasion of Hindustan," said he, "is to lead an expedition against the infidels that, according to the law of Muhammad (upon whom and his family be the blessings and peace of God), we may convert to the true faith the people of that country, and purify the land itself from the filth of infidelity and polytheism; and that we may overthrow their temples and idols and become *ghaziz* and *mujahids* before God."[1] He did his worst, and again the Hindus regained their position in the course of time. After one and a quarter century of this, when Babur invaded Hindustan, he found that "Most of the inhabitants of Hindustan are pagans. They call a pagan a Hindu... All artisans, wage-earners and officials are Hindu."[2] As late as the end of the seventeenth century, Francois Bernier also found Hindustan "a country containing hundreds of *Gentiles* to one Mogol, or even to one *Mahometan*."[3] Even when Aurangzeb from within and Nadir Shah and Abdali from without, determined to strike a final blow for Islamization of Indian population, they could not decimate the Hindus. In such a desparate situation Indian Muslims could only wistfully remember the days of Subuktigin and Mahmud of Ghazni. Muhammad Aslam in his *Farhat-un-Nazirin* says that during the Third Battle of Panipat (1761), "about ninety thousand persons, male and female, were taken prisoners, and obtained the eternal happiness by embracing the Muhammadan faith. Indeed, never was such splendid victory achieved from the time of Amir Mahmud Subuktigin..."[4] As discussed earlier, the assertion

1. *Malfuzat-i-Timuri*, E and D, III, p.397, also p.394.
2. *Babur Nama*, trs. Mrs. Beveridge, II, p.518.
3. Bernier, *Travels*, p.209.
4. Trs. in E and D, VIII, p.171.

is not correct,[1] but as a Muslim Muhammad Aslam did so will, so desire.

So, all through the medieval period, Foreign and Indian Muslims strove hard to make India a Muslim country by converting and eliminating the Hindus. They killed and converted, and converted and killed by turns. In the earlier centuries of their presence here, the picture was sombre indeed. Turkish rule was established in northern India at the beginning of the thirteenth century. Within fifteen years of Muhammad Ghori's occupation of Delhi, the Turks rapidly conquered most of the major cities of northern India. Their lightening success, as described by contemporary chroniclers, entailed great loss of life. Qutbuddin Aibak's conquests during the life-time of his master and later on in the capacity of king (c.1200-1210) included Gwalior, parts of Bundelkhand, Ajmer, Ranthambhor, Anhilwara, as well a parts of U.P. and Malwa. In Nahrwala alone 50,000 persons were killed during Aibak's campaign.[2] No wonder, he earned the nickname of killer of lacs.[3] Bakhtiyar Khalji marched through Bihar into Bengal and massacred people in both the regions. During his expedition to Gwalior Iltutmish (1210-36) massacred 700 persons besides those killed in the battle on both sides. His atttacks on Malwa (Vidisha and Ujjain) were met with stiff resistance and were accompained by great loss of life. He is also credited with killing 12,000 Khokhars (Gakkhars) during Aibak's reign.[4] The

1. K.S. Lal, *Growth of Muslim Population...*, pp.14, 154n.
2. Ferishtah, *op. cit.*, I, p.62.
3. Minhaj Siraj, *Tabqat-i-Nasiri*, Bib., Ind. (Calcutta, 1864), p.138. Also A.B.M. Habibullah, *The Foundation of Muslim Rule in India* (Allahabad, 1961), p.91.
Since most of the facts and figures for the period upto 1260 are from the *Tabqat-i-Nasiri*, references would be given only sparingly to avoid cluttering up the narrative.
4. Ferishtah, *op. cit.*, I, p.65.

successors of Iltutmish (Raziyah, Bahram, etc.) too fought and killed zealously. During the reigns of Nasiruddin and Balban (1246-86) warfare for consolidation and expansion of Turkish dominions went on apace. Trailokyavarman, who ruled over Southern U.P., Bundelkhand and Baghelkhand, and is called "Dalaki va Malaki" by Persian chroniclers, was defeated after great slaughter (1248). In 1251, Gwalior, Chanderi, Narwar and Malwa were attacked. The Raja of Malwa alone had 5,000 cavalry and 200,000 infantry and would have been defeated only after great loss of life. The inhabitants of Kaithal were given such severe punishment (1254) that they 'might not forget (the lesson) for the rest of their lives.' In 1256 Ulugh Khan Balban carried on devastating warfare in Sirmur, and 'so many of the rebellious Hindus were killed that numbers cannot be computed or described.' Ranthambhor was attacked in 1259 and 'many of its valiant fighting men were sent to hell.' In the punitive expedition to Mewat (1260) 'numberless Hindus perished under the merciless swords of the soldiers of Islam.' In the same year 12,000 men, women and children were put to the sword in Hariyana.

As a minister Balban was not soft-hearted. When he became the Sultan, he followed the policy of blood and iron, which means that his killings became even more sanguinary. His sphere of operations was, however, confined to the Ganga-Jamuna doab and Avadh, Katehar and Mewat. In Katehar large sections of the male population were massacred and, according to Barani, in villages and jungles heaps of human corpses were left rotting. During his expedition to Bengal, 'on either side of the principal bazar (of Lakhnauti) in a street two miles in length, a row of stakes was set up and the adherents of Tughril were impaled upon them.'

Alauddin Khalji and Muhammad bin Tughlaq (c. 1296-1350) were great warriors and killers. Alauddin's conquest of Gujarat (1299) and the massacres by his generals in Anhilwara, Cambay, Asavalli, Vanmanthali etc., earned him, according to the *Rasmala,* the nickname of Khuni. His contemporary chronicler proclaims that Alauddin shed more blood than the Pharaohs did.[1] He captured Ranthambhor after very heavy casualties.[2] Chittor's capture was followed by a massacre of 30,000 people, after Jauhar had been performed and the Rajputs had died fighting in large numbers. When Malwa was attacked (1305), its Raja is said to have possessed 40,000 horse and 100,000 foot.[3] After the battle, so far as human eye could see, the ground was muddy with blood.' Many cities of Malwa like Mandu, Ujjain, Dharanagari and Chanderi were captured after great resistance. The capitulation of Sevana and Jalor (1308-1311) were accompanied by massacres after years of prolonged warfare. In Alauddin's wars in the south, similar killings took place, especially in Dwarasamudra and Malabar. In the latter campaign Malik Kafur went from place to place, and to some places many times over, and in his rage at not finding the fleeing prince Vira Pandya, he killed the people mercilessely.[4] His successor Mubarak Khalji once again sacked Gujarat and Devagiri.

Under Muhammad Tughlaq, wars and rebellions knew no end. Even an enhancement of land-tax ended in massacres in the Doab. Many more perished on the way when the capital was shifted to Daulatabad. His Qarachal expedition cost him a whole army. His expeditions to Bengal, Sind and the Deccan, as well as ruthless suppression of twenty-two rebellions, meant only de-

1. Barani, *op. cit.,* pp.251-52. Isami, *op. cit.,* p.243.
   For detailed references see K.S. Lal, *History of the Khaljis,* pp.69-71.
2. For detailed reference see *Ibid.,* p.94.
3. *Ibid.,* p.113.
4. *Ibid.,* pp.252-53.

population.[1] From all accounts it is certain that in the thirteenth and first half of the fourteenth century the loss of population was immense. For one thing, in spite of constant efforts no addition of territory could be made by Turkish rulers from 1210 to 1296, for another while the weapons of the Turkish period were not as sophisticated as those of the Mughal, the Turkish rulers were more ruthless in war and less merciful towards rebels, with the result their killings were heavy. Hence the extirpating campaigns of Balban, and the repeated attacks on regions already devastated but not completely subjugated. Bengal was attacked by Bakhtiyar, by Balban, by Alauddin, and by all the three Tughlaqs – Ghayas, Muhammad and Firoz. Malwa and Gujarat were repeatedly attacked and sacked. Almost every Muslim ruler invaded Ranthambhor until it was subjugated by Alauddin Khalji (1301, again temporarily). Gwalior, Katehar and Avadh regions were also repeatedly attacked. Rajputana, Sind and Punjab (also because of the Mongol invasions), knew no peace. In the first decade of the fourteenth century Turkish invaders penetrated into the South, carrying death and destruction. When the sultans of Delhi lost their hold on the South, Bahmani and Vijayanagar kingdoms came to grips with each other. The wars between these two kingdoms generally ended in massacres. Only one instance should suffice to give an idea of this. Mulla Daud of Bidar vividly describes the fighting between Muhammad Shah Bahmani and the Vijayanagar king in 1366 in which "Ferishtah computes the victims on the Hindu side alone as numbering no less than half a million."[2] According to Ferishtah, Muhammad "So wasted the districts of Carnatic that for several decades they did not recover their natural population."[3]

1. Mahdi Hussain, *Tughlaq Dynasty*, pp.195-257.
2. Sewell, *op. cit.*, pp.30-31.
3. Ferishtah, *op. cit.*, I, p.295. Also Sewell, p.38.

Despite such killings, the Hindus could not be eliminated or reduced to a minority. Despite forcible conversions, India could not be Islamised. How did it happen? Alberuni has solved this riddle. "They (the Hindus)," says he, "differ from us in religion... There is very little disputing about theological topics among themselves; at the most they fight with words, but they will never stake their soul or body or their property on religious controvery." On the contrary "in all manners and usages they differ from us to such a degree as to frighten their children with us...and as to declare us to be devil's breed and our doings as the very opposite of all that is good and proper," so that "they call all foreigners as *mleccha,* i.e. impure, and forbid having any connection with them, be it by intermarriage or any other kind of relationship, or by sitting, eating, and drinking with them, because therby they think, they would be polluted... They are not allowed to recieve anybody who does not belong to them, even if he wished it, or was inclined to their religion."[1] In brief, the Hindus believed in peaceful disscussions about religious matters. They believed in freedom of religious thought and higher spirituality. They hated those who killed in the name of religion and they shunned those who believed in conversions.

That is how Hindu non-violence succeeded over forcible conversions; that is how culturally the Hindu won against strong and aggressive adversaries. The proof of this lies in Mughal emperor Babur's testimony. "Compared with our countries," writes he when he had settled in India, "(Hindustan) is a different world... once the water of Sind is crossed, everything is in the Hindustan way (*tariq*) – land, water, tree, rock, people and horde, opinion and custom."[2] And to repeat his words,

1. Alberuni, I, pp.19-20.
2. *Babur Nama*, p.484.

"Most of the inhabitants of Hindsutan are pagans; they call a pagan a Hindu."[1] And this after centuries of Muslim effort at changing the *dar-ul-harb* into *dar-ul-Islam*.!

The scenario has never changed to the extreme disappointment of the Indian Muslims. So that, more than anything else the endeavour of the Indian Muslims is to increase their numbers. The decadal census figures from 1881 to 1941 show a constant rise in Muslim numbers. This is a feature common with medieval times, and the pattern of modern Muslim demography can be seen in the following Table.

Table
Showing the rate of rise of Muslim population during 1881-1941

Year of the Census	Number of[2] Muslim in 000's	% age to[3] total population calculated by J.M.Datta	Inter-Censal difference	% age[4] calculation by K. Davis
1881	49, 953	19.74	--	19.97
1891	57, 068	19.96	+0.22	20.41
1901	62, 110	21.22	+1.26	21.88
1911	67, 835	21.26	+0.04	22.39
1921	71, 005	21.74	+0.48	23.23
1931	79, 306	22.16	+0.42	23.49
1941	94, 447	23.81	+1.65	24.28

1. *Ibid.*, p.518.
2. Based on the figures of K.Davis, *op. cit.*, p.193.
3. J.M. Datta, "Proportion of Mahammadans in India Through Centuries", In *Modern Review*, *op. cit.*, p.33.
4. K. Davis, *op. cit.*, p.70.

At the time of partition in 1947 the population of Indian Muslim was 9 and half crores. Millions of Muslims migrated to Pakistan, but those who stayed in India, have continued to increase at a fast rate in the following order.

Major Religious communities	Growth Rate 1951-61	Growth Rate 1961-71	Growth Rate 1971-81
Toatal population	21.51%	24.80%	24.69%
Hindus	20.29%	23.69%	24.15%
Muslims	25.61%	30.85%	30.59%
Christians	27.38%	32.60%	16.77%
Sikhs	25.15%	32.28%	26.15%
Buddhists	16.70%	17.20%	22.52%
Jains	25.17%	28.48%	23.69%

Muslims form the second largest community after the Hindus. According to the 1981 census the number of Hindus and Muslims was as follows :

Religious community	Population	% of total population
Hindus	549, 779, 481	82.64%
Muslims	75, 512, 439	11.35%

A study in some depth shows that the growth rate among the Hindus is the lowest and among Muslims the highest[1] as seen in the above Table.

1. See *The Hindustan Times*, 4 June, 1986 and *Organiser*, 23 July, 1989. Of course Census Reports provide detailed information.

Thus even in modern times at no census have the Muslim numbers failed to improve, or the Hindu failed to lose. This phenomenon has been attributed besides vigorous proselytization, to polygamy, remarriage of widows, and higher fecundity among the Muslims.[1] Kingslay Davis thinks it due to the Hindus having taken to western education and secularism with alacrity as against the general backwardness of the Muslims.[2] The insistence of the Muslims on their Personal Law, their reluctance to Family Planning, their pacts of privileges with political parties at the time of elections in particular and their receiving millions of Petro-Dollars to help in proselytizing endeavours all point to their desire and determination to grow in numbers and Islamize Hindustan. Their greatest chagrin is that in spite of their best efforts for more than a thousand years, they have ever remained a minority in India. Therefore, just as they have reconciled themselves to the peculiar circumstances of their conversion, if they could also learn to live as a minority with India's tolerant Hindu majority, there will be peace for them and for all.

1. Beni Prasad, *Modern Review*, 1921, p.17n.
   Also Hazard, *Altas of Islamic History* (Princeton, 1954), p.5.
2. Davis, *op. cit.*, p.193.

Bibliography

Contemporary Sources

Abul Fazl, Allami, *Ain-i-Akbari,* 3 vols. Vol. I translated by H. Blocmann and ed. by D.C. Phillot, Asiatic Society of Bengal (Calcutta, 1939); Vol. II trs. by H.S. Jarret and annotated by Jadunath Sarkar, A.S.B. (Calcutta, 1959); Vol. III, Jarret and Sarkar (Calcutta, 1948).

Akbar Namah. Bib. Ind. Text, 3 vols. English trs. by H. Beveridge (Calcutta, 1948).

Abdul Hamid Lahori, *Badshahnamah,* Bib. Ind., 2 vols. (Calcutta, 1898).

Afif, Shams Siraj, *Tarikh-i-Firoz Shahi,* Bib. Ind. (Calcutta, 1890).

Alberuni, Abu Raihan Muhammad, *Alberuni's India,* Eng. trs. by Edward C. Sachau, 2 vols., Trubners Oriental Series, Kegan Paul (London, 1910).

Al Biladuri, *Futuh-ul-Buldan* (Written 9th cent. C.E..) trs. in Elliot and Dowson, Vol. I.

Al Istakhri, *Kitab-ul-Aqalim* (Written C.E. 951) trs. in E and D, Vol. I.

Al Masudi, *Muruj-ul-Zuhab* (Written C.E. 941) trs. E and D, I.

Al Qalqashindi, *Subh-ul-Asha,* trs. by Otto Spies, (Aligarh, n.d.)

Amin Qazvini, *Badshah Nama,* Ms. Raza Library, Rampur.

Amir Khurd, also called Saiyyad Muhammad Kirmani, *Siyar-ul-Auliya* (Delhi, 1302 H.).

Amir Khusrau, Abul Hasan, *Deval Rani* (Aligarh, 1917); *Tughlaq Namah,* ed. Hashim Faridabadi (Aurangabad, 1933); *Ghurrat-ul-Kamal,* Pub. by Yasin Ali, Delhi. For *Khazain-ul-Futuh* see Habib.

Babur, Zahiruddin Muhammad, *Baburnamah* or *Tuzuk-i-Baburi,* trs. from Truki by Mrs. A.S. Beveridge, 2 vols., Luzac & Co. (London, 1922).

Badaoni, Abdul Qadir, ibn-i-Muluk Shah, *Muntakhab-ut-Tawarikh* ed. Ahmad Ali, Bib. Ind. (Calcutta 1868-69), Eng. trs. by Col. George S.A. Ranking, A.S.B. (Calcutta, 1898).

Baihaqi, Khvaja Abul Fazl, *Tarikh-i-Subuktagin* (Written C. 1059 C.E.) trs. in E and D, II.

Bakhtawar Khan,*Mirat-i-Alam* (Written C. 1078H/1666 C.E.) trs. E and D, VII.

Barani, Ziyauddin, *Tarikh-i-Firoz Shahi,* Bib. Ind. (Calcutta, 1862); *Sana-i-Muhammadi* , trs. in *Medieval India Quarterly,* I, pt. III.

Bihamad Khani, Muhammad, *Tarikh-i-Muhammadi,* Br. Museum Ms., Rotograph copy in Allahabad University Library.

Devalasmriti, published by Anandasrama Sanskrit Series, Poona. Eng. trs. by M.N. Ray, *Journal of the Bihar and Orissa Research Society*, 1927.

Fakhre Mudabbir, *Tarikh-i-Fakhruddin Mubarak Shah*, ed. Sir Denison Ross (London, 1927).

Fatawa-i-Alamgiri, Urdu trs. Nawal Kishore Press, Lucknow.

Ferishtah, Muhammad Qasim Hindu Shah, *Gulshan-i-Ibrahimi*, also known as *Tarikh-i-Ferishtah*, Persian text, Nawal Kishore Press (Lucknow, 1865).

Firoz Shah Tughlaq, *Fatuhat-i-Firoz Shahi* (Aligarh, 1943).

Ibn Battutah, *The Rehla of Ibn Battutah*, Eng. trs. by Agha Mahdi Husain, Oriental Institute (Baroda, 1953).

Ibn Batoutah's Voyages ed. C. Defremery and B.R. Sanguinetti (Paris, 1857).

Ibn Haukal, *Ashkalal-ul-Bilad* (Written 976 C.E.), trs. E and D, I.

Ibn-ul-Asir, Shaikh Abul Hasan Ali, *Kamil-ut-Tawarikh*, (Written C. 12th century C.E.) trs. E and D, II.

Idrisi, *Nuzhat-ul-Mushtaq* (Written 12th century C.E.), trs., E and D, I.

Isami, Khvaja Abdullah Malik., *Futuh-us-Salatin*, ed. Agha Mahdi Husain, Educational Press (Agra, 1938).

Jamali, Hamid Ibn Fazl Allah, *Siyar-ul-Arifin* (Delhi, 1311 H).

Kalhana, *Rajtarangini*, trs. M.A. Stein (Westminster, 1900).

Kamboh, Muhammad Saleh, *Amil Saleh*, Bib. Ind., 3 vols. (Calcutta, 1923, 1927, 1939)

Kanz-ul-Mahfuz (Written C. 1150 H.), trs. E and D, VIII.

Khafi Khan, Muhammad Hashim, *Muntakhab-ul-Lubab*, ed. Kabiruddin Ahmad, Bib. Ind. (Calcutta 1869, 1925).

Khan, Ali Muhammad, *Mirat-i-Ahmadi* trs. by Lokhandwala, Oriental Institute (Baroda, 1965).

Lahori, See Abdul Hamid.

Mir Masum, *Tarikh-i-Masumi* also called *Tarikh-i-Sindh*, ed.Daudpota, Bhandarkar Oriental Research Institute (Poona, 1938).

Minhaj Siraj Jurjani, *Tabqat-i-Nasiri*, Bib. Ind. (Calcutta, 1864) Eng. trs. by Major H.R. Raverty (London, 1881).

Muhammad Aslam, *Farhat-un-Nazirin* (Written C.E. 1770-71) trs. in E and D, VIII.

Muhammad Sharif Hanafi, *Majalis-us-Salatin* trs. E and D, VII.

Mustaad Khan Saqi, *Maasir-i-Alamgiri* trs. and annotated by Jadunath Sarkar, R.A.S. Bengal (Calcutta, 1947).

Nizamuddin Ahmad, *Tabqat-i-Akbari*, Bib. Ind., 3 vols. (Calcutta, 1927-35) and trs. by B. De.

Nurul Haqq. *Zabdut-Tawarikh* (Written close of Akbar's reign) trs. E and D, VI.

Price, Major David, trs. of *Tarikh-i-Salim Shahi* under the title of "Memoirs of the Emperor Jahangueir, written by himself " (London, 1829) Indian edition, Bangabasi Press, (Calcutta, 1906).
Qazvini, See Amin.
Ranking, See Badaoni.
Razi, Amin Ahmad, *Haft Aqlim*, ed. A.H. Hatley, Abdul Muqtadir, and M. Mahfuzul Haq, Bib., Ind. (Calcutta, 1939).
Reynolds, See Utbi.
Rizqullah Mushtaqi, *Waqiat-i-Mushtaqi*, Photograph copy of the British Museum Ms. Ad. 11, 633.
Shaikh Abdul Haqq Dehlvi, *Akbar-ul-Akhiyar* (Delhi, 1309 H).
Shihabuddin Abul Abbas Ahmad, *Masalik-ul-Absar fi Mumalik-ul-Amsar* (Written C. middle 14th century),trs. in E and D, III and Rizvi, *Tughlaq Kalin Bharat*.
Sijzi, Amir Hasan, *Favaid-ul-Fuad* (Delhi, 1856).
Sirat-i-Firoz Shahi, anonymous. Mss. Bankipore and Allahabad University.
Sikandar bin Muhammad, *Mirat-i-Sikandari* (Bombay, 1308 H)
Sujan Rai, *Khulsat-ut-Tawarikh*, ed. Zafar Hasan (Delhi, 1918).
Sulaiman Saudagar, trs. from Arabic into Hindi, the narrative of Sulaiman the Merchant by Munshi Mahesh Prasad, Nagari Pracharini Sabha (Kashi, Sam. 1978, C.E. 1921).
Tarikh-i-Salim Shahi, see Price.
Timur, Amir, *Mulfuzat-i-Timuri*, trs. in E and D, III and Urdu trs.
Tuzuk-i-Jahangiri or Memoirs of Emperor Jahangir, trs. by Rogers and Beveridge, photo reprint (Delhi, 1968).
Utbi, Abu Nasr Muhammad, *Kitab-i-Yamini*, trs. by James Reynolds (London, 1868) also under *Tarikh-i-Yamini* in E and D, II.
Wassaf, Abdullah, *Tajziyat-ul-Amsar va Tajriyat-ul-Asar*, also called *Tarikh-i-Wassaf* (Written C. 1327), (Bombay, 1877).
Yahiya Sarhindi, *Tarikh-i-Mubarak Shahi*, Bib., Ind. (Calcutta, 1931).
Yazdi, Sharafuddin, *Zafar Namah*, 2 vols. Bib., Ind. (Calcutta, 1885-88).
Zakaria al-Qazvini, *Asar-ul-Bilad* (Written just after the middle of the 13th century), trs. E and D, I.

Travellers' Accounts

Barbosa, Durate, *The Book of Duarte Barbosa*, 2 vols., Hakluyt Society (London, 1918-21).
Bernier, Francois, *Travels in the Mogul Empire*, revised by V.A. Smith, Archibald Constable (Oxford, 1934).
Du Jarric, *Akbar and the Jesuits*, see Payne.

Eden, Richard., *The First Book of the Historie of the Discoverie and Conquest of the East Indies by the Portingals* (London, 1582), contains trs. of Castanheda's account.

Finch, William, see Foster.

Foster, W., *Early Travels in India* (1583-1619), contains narratives of Fitch (pp. 1-47), Mildenhall (pp. 48-59), Hawkins (pp. 60-121), Finch (122-187), Withington (pp. 188-233), Coryat (pp. 234-87) and Terry (pp. 288-322) (London, 1927).

————*English Factories in India* (1618-69) 13 vols. (Oxford, 1906-27).

Hakluyt, Richard, *Principal Navigations, Voyages, Traffiques, and Discoveries of the English Nation* (Glasgow, 1903-05).

Heber, Reginald, *Narrative of a Journey through the Upper Provinces of India*, second ed., 3 vols., (London, 1828).

Major, R.H., *India in the Fifteenth Century* (contains extracts from narratives of Nicolo Conti, Santo Stefano etc.), Hakluyt Society (London, 1857).

Mandelslo, *Mandelslo's Travles in Western India* by M.S. Commissariat (London, 1931).

Manrique, *Travels of Frey Sebastian Manrique*, trs. by Eckford Luard, 2 vols., Hakluyt Society(London, 1927).

Manucci, Niccolao, *Storia do Mogor* Eng. trs. by W. Irvine, 4 vols., John Murray (London, 1906).

Marco Polo, see Yule.

Marshall, *John Marshall in India* (1668-72) ed. Shafaat Ahmed Khan (London, 1927).

Payne, C.H., *Akbar and the Jesuits*, contains in trs. Du Jarric's account of the Jesuit Missions to the Court of Akbar (London, 1926).

Tavernier, *Travels in India*, trs. and ed. by V. Ball (London, 1925).

Thevenot, *Indian Travels of Thevenot and Careri*, ed. by Surendra Nath Sen (New Delhi, 1949).

Varthema, *The Itinerary of Ludovico di Varthema of Bologna* ed. by Sir Richard Temple (London, 1928).

Yule, Sir Henry, and H. Cordier, *The Book of Ser Marco Polo*, 2 vols. (New York, 1903).

Modern Works

Abdul Karim, *Social Hisotry of the Muslims in Bengal*, Asiatic Society of Pakistan (Dacca, 1959).

Abdur Rashid, Shaikh, *Najib-ud-daulah, His Life and Times*, Cosmopolitan Publishers (Aligarh, 1952).

Ahmad, Nafis, "The Evolution of the Boundaries of EastPakistan", in the *Oriental Geographer*, II, No. 2, July, 1958.

Ahmad Shah, *Bijak of Kabir* (Hamirpur, 1917).
Arnold, T.W., *The Preaching of Islam* (Westminster, 1896).
Aziz Ahmad, *Studies in Islamic Culture in the Indian Environment* (Oxford, 1964).
Beni Prasad, "India in A.C. 1605" in *Modern Review*, Calcutta, January, 1921.
———*A History of Jahangir*, Third ed., The Indian Press (Allahabad, 1940)
Biswas, Satya Krishna, *Banshasmriti* (Bengali) (Calcutta, 1926).
Bosworth, C.E., *The Ghaznavids*, Edinburgh University Press(Edinburgh, 1963).
The Cambridge History of India
Vol. I, Ed. by Raspon, Camb. University Press, 1922;
Vol. III, Ed. by Wolseley Haig, Reprint (Delhi, 1958);
Vol. IV, Ed. by Sir Richard Burn, (Cambridge, 1937);
Vol. V, Ed. by Dodwell, Reprint, (Delhi, 1963).
Census of India Reports, 1901, 1921 and 1931, Vol. 18, United Provinces, Part 2.
Colin Clark, *Population Growth and Land Use*, Macmillan (New York, 1967).
Crooke, W. *Tribes and Castes of North Western Provinces*, 4 vols.
Cunha, T.B., *Goa's Freedom Struggle* (Bombay, 1967).
Currie, P.M. *The Shrine and Cult of Muin-ul-din Chishti of Ajmer*, Oxford (Delhi, 1989)
Datta, Jatindra Mohan, "Proportion of Muhammadans in India Through Centuries" in *Modern Review*, Calcutta, January, 1948.
Davis, Kingsley, *The Population of India and Pakistan*, Princeton, (New Jersey, 1951).
Day, U.N., *Medieval Malwa*, Munshiram Manoharlal (Delhi, 1965).
Denison Ross, *Islam*.
Dorn, Benhard, *History of the Afghans*, being trs. of the *Makhzan-i-Afghana*, Oriental Translation Fund (London, 1829).
Eaton, Richard Maxwell, *Sufis of Bijapur* 1300-1700 (Princeton, 1978).
Elliot, H.M. and J. Dowson, *History of India as Told by itsown Historians*, 8 vols. (London, 1867-77).
Encyclopaedia Britannica, Eleventh Edition.
Encyclopaedia of Social Sciences, Macmillan, 1949 Reprint.
Fazle Karim, See Rabbi.
Francklin, W., *A History of the Reign of Shah-Aulum*, first pub., 1798 (Allahabad, 1915).
Fuhrer, and Smith, *The Sharqi Architecture of Jaunpur* (Calcutta, 1889).

Goyal, "A Survey of Fertility and Family Planning in Western Uttar Pradesh", Demographic Research Centre, Institute of Economic Growth, Delhi (Mimeo)

Habib, Mohammad, *Sultan Mahmud of Ghaznin* (Delhi reprint, 1951).

———*Some Aspects of the Foundation of the Delhi Sultanate,* K.M. Ashfaf Memorial Lecture (Delhi, 1966).

———*Khazain-ul-Futuh's* Eng. trs. under the title of *Campaigns of Alauddin Khalji* (Bombay, 1933).

Habibullah, A.B.M., *The Foundation of Muslim Rule in India,* Revised ed. (Allahabad, 1961). First published Lahore, 1945.

Hall, D.G.E., *A History of South East Asia,* Macmillan & Co. (London, 1955).

Hazard, H.W., *Atlas of Islamic History* (Princeton, 1954).

Hodivala, S.H., *Studies in Indo-Muslim History* (Bombay, 1939).

Hughes, T.P., *Dictionary of Islam,* W.H. Allen & Co. (London, 1885).

Indian Antiquary

Indian Historical Quarterly

Indian History Congress Proceedings

Indian Heritage, Vol. I, Bharatiya Vidya Bhavan (Bombay, 1955).

Ira Mervin Lapidus, *Muslim Cities in the Later Middle Ages* (Cambridge, Mass, 1967).

Ishwari Prasad, *A History of the Quraunah Turks in India,* Vol. I, The Indian Press (Allahabad, 1936).

———*Medieval India,* fourth impression (Allahabad, 1940).

Ivanow, W., *Brief Survey of Evolution of Ismailism* (Bombay, 1942).

Journal of the Asiatic Society of Bengal.

Kane, P.V., *History of Dharmashastra,* 5 vols. (Poona, 1930-58).

Karim, A.K. Nazmul, "Muslim Social Classes of East Pakistan", in *Changing Society in India and Pakistan,* University of Dacca (1956).

Kennedy, Melville T., *The Chaitanya Movement* (Calcutta, 1925).

Khan, Abdul Majid, "Research About Muslim Aristocracy in East Pakistan" in Pierre Bessaignet ed. *Social Research in East Pakistan,* Asiatic Society of Pakistan (Dacca, 1960).

Kirk, Dudley, "Factors Affecting Muslim Natality" in Olivia Schieffelin ed. *Muslim Attitude Towards Family Planning,* Demographic Division, The Population Council, Inc. (New York, 1967).

Lach, Donald F., *Asia in the Making of Europe,* Vol. I, Bks. I and II (Chicago, 1965).

——— Lach Tabels see Appendix.

Lal, K.S., *History of the Khaljis,* Asia Publishing House (Bombay, 1967) First Pub., 1950.

———*Twilight of the Sultanate,* Asia (Bombay, 1963).

———*Studies in Medieval Indian History*, Ranjit Publisher (Delhi, 1966).

———*Growth of Muslim Population in Medieval India*, Research Publications in Social Sciences (New Delhi, 1973).

——— *Early Muslims in India* (New Delhi, 1984).

———*The Mughal Harem*, Aditya Prakashan, (New Delhi, 1988).

Lanepoole, Stanely, *Medieval India under Muhammadan Rule*, First Pub. 1903, T. Fisher Unwin (London, 1926).

Levy, Ruben, *The Social Structure of Islam* (Cambridge, 1957).

Logan, W., *Malabar* (Madras, 1951).

Macauliffe, Max Arthur, *The Sikh Religion, its Gurus, Sacred Writings and Authors*, 6 vols. (Oxford, 1909).

Mahalanbois, P.C., "Distribution of Muslims in the Population of India : 1941" in *Sankhya, The Indian Journal of Statistics*, Calcutta, Vol. VII, August, 1945.

Mahdi Husain, *Tughluq Dynasty*, Thacker, Spink & Co. (Calcutta, 1963).

Majumdar, D.N. and Rao, C.R., *Race Elements in Bengal*, Asia Publishing House (Bombay, 1970).

Majumdar R.C., "Study of Indian History", *Journal of the Bombay Branch of the Asiatic Society*, 1957.

——— (ed.),*The Struggle for Empire* (Bombay, 1957)

——— (ed.),*The Delhi Sultanate* (Bombay, 1960).

Mazumdar B.P., *The Socio-Economic History of Northern India* (Calcutta, 1960)

Misra, S.C., *Muslim Communities in Gujarat*, Asia Pub. House (Bombay, 1964).

———*The Rise of Muslim Power in Gujarat*, Asia Pub. House (Bombay, 1954).

Mitra, R.C., *The Decline of Buddhism in India* (Visvabharati, 1954).

Modern Cyclopaedia, 8 vols. (London, 1901).

Mujeeb, M., *The Indian Muslims*, Gerorge Allen and Unwin (London, 1967).

Orme, Robert, *A History of the Military Transactions of the British Nation in Indostan*, 3 vols., Fourth Edition, (London, 1803).

Qanungo, K.R., *Historical Essays* (Agra, 1968).

Qureshi, Ishtiaq Hussain., *The Muslim Community in the Indo-Pakistan Subcontinent*, Monton & Co., 'S--Gravenhage, 1962.

Rabbi, Dewan Fazle, *The Origin of the Muhammadans of Bengal*, Thacker, Spink & Co. (Calcutta, 1895).

Ram Gopal, *Indian Muslims, A Political History (1858-1947)*, Asia Publishing House, (Bombay, 1959.)

Ram Swarup, *Understanding Islam thorugh Hadis*, Voice of India, (New Delhi, Reprint 1984).

Rao, R.P., *Portuguese Rule in Goa*, Asia Pub. House (Bombay, 1963).

Raverty, H.G., *Notes on Afghanistan* (London, 1886). Also see Minhaj under Contemporary Sources.

Report of the Indian Historical Records Commision, Vol. V, 1923.

Risley, H.H., *The Tribes and Castes of Bengal*, Bengal Secretariat Press (Calcutta, 1891).

Rizvi, A.A., *Muslim Revivalist Movements in Northern India in the Sixteenth and Seventeenth Centuries*, Agra University (Agra, 1965).

————*Tughlaq Kalin Bharat*, Aligarh, Part I, 1956, Part II, 1957.

———— *Uttar Timur Kalin Bharat*, Part II, (Aligarh, 1959.)

Saran, Parmatma, *Resitance of Indian Princes to Turkish Offensive*, Sita Ram Kohli Memorial Lectures, Punjabi University (Patiala, 1967).

Sarkar, Jadunath, *History of Aurangzeb*, 5 vols. (Calcutta 1912-1925).

————*Fall of the Mughal Empire*, 4 vols., Third Ed. (Calcutta, 1964).

———— *Later Mughals* (ed. Irvine) 2 vols. (Calcutta, 1921-22).

———— *History of Bengal*, 2 vols., Dacca, 1948.

Sen, D.C., *Chaitanya and His Age* (Calcutta, 1922).

————*History of Bengali Language and Literature*, Calcutta University (Calcutta, 1911).

Sen, Sukumar, *Bangla Sahityer Itihasa* (Calcutta, 1940).

Sewell, Robert, *A Forgotton Empire* (Vijayanagar), Publications Division (Delhi, 1962).

Sharma, Sri Ram, *The Religious Policy of the Mughal Emperors*, Asia Publishing House (Bombay, 1962).

————*Conversion and Re-conversion to Hinduism*, D.A.V. College Hisotrical Series, No. 2. n.d.

Sherwani, H.K., *Mahmud Gawan*, Kitabistan (Allahabad, 1942).

————*The Bahmanis of the Deccan* (Hyderabad, n.d.)

Smith, V.A., *Akbar the Great Mogul* (Delhi, Reprint, 1962).

Tara Chand, *Influence of Islam on Indian Culture*, The Indian Press (Allahabad, 1946).

Titus, Murray, *Islam in India and Pakistan* (Calcutta, 1959).

Thronton, Edward, *Gazetteer of the Territories under the Government of the East India Co. and of the Native States on the Continent of India, Complied by the authority of the Court of Directors and chiefly from the documents in their possession*, 4 vols. Wm. H. Allen & Co. (London, 1854).

Tripathi, R.P., *Some Aspects of Muslim Administration*, The Indian Press (Allahabad, 1936).

Wahid Mirza, *Life and Times of Amir Khusrau* (Calcutta, 1935).

Westcott, *Kabir and the Kabir Panth* (Cawnpore, 1907).

Index of Names and Subjects